Musings

from Me and My Master

Bob Morley

Musings from Me and My Master

Dedication

**This book is dedicated to my wife, Barbara.
Sent from God.**

Contents

Musings?

Webster's Dictionary defines a "musing" as "something to meditate on." One of the things I meditate on quite often is how the Holy Spirit nudges Christians to be His hands and mouth in this world we live in. Most times it is a gentle nudge. But occasionally it seems almost like a shove. These nudgings may be as simple as to pray, or to read our Bible. But sometimes they are to say something, or help someone, or even occasionally to do something quite drastic. And often it seems like the tasks might be better served by someone else with more ability for the situation we are nudged into.

In my case, the nudgings seem to end with me sitting at this computer, typing things that hopefully will help open someone up to the drawing of the Holy Spirit, either to make Jesus the Lord of their life, or in the case of existing Christians, to bring them into an even closer relationship with their Savior. In many ways this is almost comical in that since I never learned how to type, I peck away at the keyboard with my one right index finger. Reason would suggest that I would be one of the last people to be nudged into sitting at this keyboard. But as the saying goes, "God is not after our ability, but our availability."

At any rate, for several years I have been blessed beyond my wildest imagination to hear that the words that end up on my computer screen after a session of hunting and pecking have in fact had an impact on so many who happened to read them. Readers have often written letters or e-mail that bring tears of joy to my eyes. Obviously none of the credit for lives changed belongs to me. It is always the Holy Spirit who draws people to the Lord.

Oh, I'm sure that a lot of the thoughts and words that I type come from me, but sometimes I'm not so certain. In fact, often when my one finger starts searching for a letter on the keyboard, I have very little idea of what might be in the very next sentence, or where the train of thought is really going. I could never be the poster child for a writer's training conference. I have even realized that on occasions when I sat down with a bunch of notes to work from, words just seemed to come, and in the end, none of the notes were even used. The end result had nothing whatsoever to do with the notes. I have even had the phenomenal experience of reading over what I had typed only to find to my amazement that what I thought I was going to type, and what I thought I knew about a subject, had dramatically changed in the course of the typing.

Can I prove that the Holy Spirit has nudged me to get me to write something, or that He graciously led me in what to write? No. I can't. In Unlocking God's Secrets I firmly believe that God's existence was completely proven. And responses from former atheists seem to lend credence to that fact. But proving that the Holy Spirit is in any way involved with what I type is obviously illusive. I can say that I pray for his help virtually each time I strike the first key on the keyboard. And I do believe strongly in the power of prayer. I believe God listens to us, and answers.

I also believe that the Holy Spirit often leads us to watch something, or be at a certain place at a certain time, or to read something. And if He does lead us, it is to draw us closer to our Master, or to help a fellow traveler in this temporary world draw closer. My hope is that there is something within the following black and white words, typed with one finger on the following pages, that the Holy Spirit specifically wants you to read, either for your benefit or for someone you might share it with.

The selection within this book is a combination of many things. Some are brand new things that were written specifically for this book. These things talk about varied and exciting new tid bits that I have just learned. A few are much more dramatic than just tid bits. Then again, some of the selections were ones that seemed to touch readers the most when they were first included on at www.unlockinggodssecrets.com. There are even a few that were originally just e-mail that I sent to one or more people. All of them, though, quite naturally deal in some regard with God. He is my passion.

The topics are wide ranging, from obscure Biblical verses to ordinary daily living. Some deal with prophecies. Some with types and shadows that I don't think have ever been explored in a book before. Some deal with the natural, while some others with the supernatural. Each article stands alone. Very few have any relation to another one other than the underlying majesty and wonder of our Creator and His Word. But through this roller coaster journey, I pray that you will find out things you didn't already know about your loving Father. Things about His nature, His plan, and His never ending focus on you. And I hope you will have some moments when you say, "Wow."

My desire is that you will find plenty of things to meditate on in the following selections. And I pray that something you will read will strike a chord in your heart. Thank you so much for joining me in these <u>Musings from Me and My Master</u>.

To Meet The President

A Union soldier heard the terrible news that both his father and his only brother were tragically killed at Gettysburg. His thoughts immediately went to his sister back home. How could she possibly take care of the farm work and bring in the harvest all by herself? After getting permission, he traveled to Washington to see if President Lincoln would give him a discharge to let him go home to help his sister take care of the farm.

Unfortunately, when he reached the White House he was turned away by a guard who told him that the president was much too busy to see him. Disheartened and dejected, the young man walked across the street and sat on a park bench.

A boy walked up to him and asked, "Why are you so sad?"

So the young soldier poured his heart out to the little boy. After hearing the story the boy extended his hand and said, "Come with me."

The soldier took the little boy's hand and followed him back to the White house, past the guards who this time were silent, and straight into the office of President Abraham Lincoln. They did not even knock on the office door. Lincoln looked up from the battle plans he and a general were discussing and asked, "Who is your friend, Todd?"

"He is a soldier who needs help, and Dad, you are the only person who can help him," said young Todd Lincoln.

With that introduction the soldier told his story and immediately was given a discharge and allowed to go to his family home.

Incredible as it may sound, by taking the hand of Jesus the Son, you and I are ushered directly into the throne room of His Father, the King of everything. We are immediately given our discharge from our past sins, and are allowed to go back to our heavenly home. The true story of Todd Lincoln and the soldier is a mere earthly imitation of the even more exciting heavenly reality.

The Shadow of the Song

As wonderful as the surface message in God's Word is, I am even more in awe of the types and shadows that the Creator of everything lovingly hid beneath the surface for us to find like nuggets of gold hidden beneath the sandy bottom of a babbling brook. One of the most beautiful is one that is hidden in the seldom read book that use to be called Song of Solomon, but more recently has been named the Song of Songs.

It is a shame that virtually no one ever hears a message taught on this love story anymore, because it is the one book in the Bible that should make a follower of Jesus tingle all over. Unfortunately, most people just push the book to the side as only being a love poem from Solomon to his cherished love. Some people think about the book as being a picture of the way a mortal man and his wife should perceive each other. In reality, though, the deeper meaning, the spiritual meaning, is the one God wants us to fully understand. Song of Songs is the most incredible picture of the love Jesus has for us, His bride to be.

To uncover the treasure of the shadow I want to briefly discuss, lets look first at Matthew 24:32-33, in which Jesus, talking about the end times, says, *"Now learn a parable of the fig tree; When his branch is yet tender, and putteth forth leaves, ye know that summer is nigh: So likewise ye, when ye shall see all these things, know that it is near, even at the doors."* (KJV) The interesting thing is that every other time Jesus told His listeners to learn of a parable, he went into a long story about something. In this case, however, He didn't. That was probably because He knew that His listeners were familiar with the parable already. If we go back to the Old Testament to search out what they may have been familiar with, the mention of a fig tree that stands out as similar is in Song of Songs 2:13, *"The fig tree putteth forth her green figs, and the vines with the tender grape give a good smell."* (KJV) That is our clue that the second chapter of Song of Songs is also talking about the end times, just like Matthew 24.

In Song of Songs 2:8 the bride to be says, *"Look! Here he comes, leaping across the mountains, bounding over the hills."* (NIV) Did you happen to notice that he does not touch down on earth? Ponder that. It is the same with the rapture. The love story goes on in verse 10 with, *"My lover spoke and said to me, 'Arise, my darling, my beautiful one, and come with me."* (NIV) But then interestingly the verse is repeated almost verbatim again in verse 13 with, *"Arise, come, my darling; my beautiful one, come with me."* (NIV)

Could the reason the love call to arise was repeated twice be that there are two groups that make up the bride? I believe so. And I believe the explanation and the exciting answer for this question within this phenomenal shadow of love is found in 1 Thessalonians 4:16-18, *"For the Lord himself will come down from heaven, with a loud command, with the voice of the archangel and with the trumpet call of God, and the dead in Christ will rise first. After that, we who are still alive and are left will be caught up together with them in the clouds to meet the Lord in the air. And so we will be with the Lord forever. Therefore encourage each other with these words."* (NIV)

Yes, we talk about the rapture as being God's way of taking Christ's bride to be out of harms way before the wrath of the Tribulation comes. But it is much more than that to Jesus. It is a big part of a passionate love story foretold in the beautiful little book, Song of Songs, too often overlooked. Read it again yourself. It is the ultimate love letter, and Jesus penned it entirely for you.

Naturally Supernatural

It is interesting to find that God uses what He created "in the beginning" to orchestrate what we at first glance think of as supernatural. For instance, geologists have now found archaeological evidence that proves that the cities of Sodom and Gomorrah were actually destroyed by a volcano thousands of years ago. A natural "supernatural" event.

Of course, we look at future prophecies and immediately jump to the conclusion that God is going to have to use supernatural occurrences to bring them about. In reality, He will again use the natural to perform what we think of as supernatural. Let's look briefly at two of those exciting future events.

We know that when Jesus comes back to earth to stop the Battle of Armageddon he will set foot on the Mount of Olives, from which He ascended. When He does, the mountain will split in two. In fact, Zechariah 14:4 tells us, *"On that day His feet will stand on the mount of Olives, east of Jerusalem, and the Mount of Olives will split in two from east to west, forming a great valley, with half of the mountain moving north and half moving south."*

In the past few years we have learned that an event like that is already getting ready to happen. Interestingly, a large hotel chain was planning to build a new hotel on the Mount of Olives but had to change their plans when the ground tests showed that the area was way too unstable, due to a fault line running under the mountain. An impending earthquake seems to be developing. As Gomer Pile would say, "Surprise, surprise."

Also fascinating to me is the fact that a large underground lake under Jerusalem has recently been discovered. We all know that Ezekiel tells in his description of the millennial temple in chapter 47 that, *"I saw water coming out from under the threshold of the temple toward the east."* This water is then described as becoming a river that will flow toward the Dead Sea. Obviously when the natural earthquake occurs when Jesus returns, the underground lake will be released, and since the Dead Sea is the lowest point on the earth, 1,378 feet below sea level, the water will just naturally wind its way down to it. What did Gomer Pile say?

God's creation was perfect for carrying out His final purpose. We are reminded that in the end, it is all about God. It is not all about us.

Our God is too awesome for words.

The Prayer Of Faith

We read in the Bible *"The prayer offered in faith will make the sick person well."* James 5:15. That is exciting. But what exactly is the prayer of faith? And how do we know if we pray one? Could it be that the answer to these two questions would change our entire lives? I believe that could be true, so let's try to dig out the answers.

Unfortunately our prayers more times than not are just prayers of asking, not prayers of faith. Often, if we are honest with ourselves, our supplications when we approach God are prayers of "unfaith," or at best, "very, very little faith." The truth is that we many times pray "prayers of hope" that don't even come close to "prayers of faith." What a slap in the face to God.

The Bible tells us in Hebrews 11:6 that *"without faith it is impossible to please God,"* so we might as well realize right up front that if we pray a prayer without true faith it probably won't ever be answered. We haven't pleased God. But where do we get this faith that pleases God? Pastor Shaumback once said that if we don't get answers to prayers it is because we have forgotten one of the "P's": **His presence, His power,** or **His promises**. Most of us always remember His presence and His power. That means then that it must be in remembering His promises that we normally fall short. Remember, God can't break a promise, so if we forget His promises, or worse, don't even know them, we have totally missed one of the three cornerstone "P's." This is where daily, serious Bible study comes into play. This requires work, but the ability to truly pray a prayer of faith is well worth the time spent reading the phenomenally exciting letter from God, His Word.

To go a step further, we are also told in James 5:16 that "*the prayer of a righteous man is powerful and effective.*" Years ago when I started pondering that scripture, I knew I wanted to become "righteous" so that my prayers would be effective for the people I was praying for. The problem was that I didn't know at that time what God's definition of "righteous" was. I knew what man's idea of being righteous was, but I wanted to know God's definition. I began a search of the Bible. The only thing I could find that was close to a definition was the scripture, "*Abraham believed God and it was credited to him as righteousness.*" Romans 4:3. So there it was, to be righteous we need to **believe** God. Once again, we need to know what God says before we can believe Him. That takes us back to studying the Bible.

Once we know God's promises, and are sure of His presence and power, things begin to change in our prayer life. We then start to truly believe. Matthew 21:22 says, "*If you believe you will receive whatever you ask for in prayer.*" What a promise that is! On the other hand, God is very clear about the fact that if we have doubts we should not even expect our prayers to be answered. He says that a man that has doubts, "*is like the waves of the sea tossed to and fro ... he is a double minded ma*n. *He should not believe that he will receive anything from*

God." James 1:6-8.

In the above we are getting a picture of what the prayer of faith is, but how do we know if we have prayed one. Smith Wigglesworth, one of the most powerful men of prayer of all time, said that "the fifth prayer is definitely a prayer of unbelief." What he was trying to tell us was that if we pray, and then feel we have to pray the second time, we must not believe God has begun the manifestation of the answer. If we then pray again, even more doubt has crept in. By the fifth prayer we are in total unbelief. In Smith Wigglesworth's case, he prayed for the dead to be raised up, and they were.

Now, I know that some will argue and tell me that the story in Luke 18 of the persistent widow proves that we should keep praying no matter what. And I understand that argument fully. But doesn't it make sense that the second and subsequent prayers should be prayers of thanks to God that He has answered the initial prayer, and that the answer is definitely on the way, and not another prayer of supplication?

The answer then to how we know if we've prayed a prayer of faith is whether or not we feel that we need to pray for something again. If we've prayed a prayer of faith, we just have a ***knowing*** that the problem is solved. We don't have to even think about it again. It is then that we trust God. And it is then that miracles happen.

If we get off our knees with only hope, not true faith, we had better get back down on our knees and start all over. Our God is a miracle working God, but it is *"If we believe, we will receive."* Matthew 21:22.

Fascinating Timing

In <u>Unlocking God's Secrets</u> we spent time looking at how detailed God is in His order of things, and how interested He seems to be in numbers. We even talked about God's definition of each number. There is a fascinating example of God's repetition of numbers that we did not discuss in the book that I think you will find very intriguing.

Have you have ever wondered why God was so detailed in His Word as to even give us the ages of fathers when their children were born? If so, this will amaze you. What I am alluding to is the Biblical fact that there were 130 years between Adam and Seth, 105 years between Seth and Enos, 90 years between Enos and Cainan, etc. Every single generational gap from Adam to Abram's birth is listed in numbers of years.

When we add up the years between all those generations we come to a grand total of 1,948 years. Now, when we look at the period from Jesus to the rebirth of Israel as a nation in 1948 we obviously come up with the same 1,948 years.

God orchestrated the timing of these two events to be exactly the same. The time from the first Adam to the creation of the Hebrew nation was identical to the timing from the second Adam (Jesus) to the creation of the second Hebrew nation, Israel.

God is utterly awesome!

Joy

Jim was madly in love. He had been off fighting the British in the war of independence, and his life had been spared. He had survived a close call, and he had been saved. Now, all he could think of was getting home to his beloved wife. By day he thought about her. By night, she was in his dreams.

All that remained was crossing Laurel mountain and he would hold her in his arms. Joy consumed him. Even the troubles he encountered crawling through the miles of the thick laurel bushes for which the mountain was named could not lessen that joy. Even the many scratches from the briars that were everywhere did nothing to sway his anticipation. The only one who really mattered to him was on the other side of Laurel Mountain. The anticipation mounted. A grin was on his face, no matter what small obstacles confronted him. He endured the small sufferings for a little while, knowing the supreme joy that was his on the other side.

You and I should be Jim. But are we? We, too, have been saved, and are on the last leg of the journey to be with the one we love. So, where is the joy?

God's Word tells us, *"Let us fix our eyes on Jesus, the author and perfecter of our faith, who for the joy set before Him endured the cross..."* Hebrews 12:2. Jesus went through what He did *"for the joy set before Him."*

So why are we not bubbling over with joy with what is ahead of us? We face a few laurel thickets or a briar or two and alas, woe is us. Maybe the problem is that we are way too short sighted. We look at the saving aspect of what we have been given, and we see that as the end. Dear reader, that is just the beginning. Jim didn't stay on the battlefield where he was saved. No way. Jim's joy was just beginning, and he knew it. He was on his way home to his beloved. You couldn't wipe that grin off his face. No pesky briars could take away his joy.

We should view the rest of our earthly lives the same way. Yes, we have been saved, but our beloved awaits us at the end of our walk home. We should be grinning like mules eating briars, not solemn and whiny because a little briar pricked us.

The only place in the Bible that I have found where God actually tells us His will for our lives is found in 1 Thessalonians 5:16-18, *"Be joyful always; pray continually; give thanks in all circumstances, for this is God's will for you in Christ Jesus."*

The first of the three things listed in God's will for our lives is that we **be joyful always.**

OK. So let's put smiles on our faces. And let's leave them there, day and night. The world can be cranky, irritable, and whiny and worried about every little thing. They deserve to be. They have no joy ahead of them.

But us, we are on our way to joy unthinkable. We need to act like it. God expects no less from us.

The Martinique Shadow

For a truly exciting journey, let's look at what may be one of the most incredible events of modern time. I promise that you will be totally amazed, so much so that you will probably never forget this reading. One of the most startling things to me about this story, and there are many, is that although it occurred only about a hundred years ago, and was front page news around the world for months, very few of our generation even know about it. Ponder what could be the reason for this as you read it. That in itself may cause you to shudder.

In my book, <u>Unlocking God's Secrets</u>, we looked at many exciting "shadows" of things to come that were orchestrated by God in actual historical events. The question for today is whether or not God stopped orchestrating events to show similar shadows, or is He still doing the same thing in modern times. We must remember that the stories we study in the Bible as shadows of things that were to come were actual historical events.

Please know that I have spent many hours researching what I am about to share with you, to the point of going over such things as old newspaper accounts of the events, and I will tell you that as astonishing as parts of this story may sound, everything I will write did in fact happen. I hope you are seated firmly, because you are about to be blown away.

Our story begins on the beautiful Caribbean island

of Martinique in 1902. Although traditional Catholic and Protestant churches had been a part of that French island's culture for many years, what few Christian believers remained had become quite apathetic towards the majority view which held that the Christian religion was out of date. The dwindling population of believers could be described as luke warm at best. Most of the citizens either did not believe in God at all, or if they did believe He existed, He had just become an object for ridicule and mockery.

There was, however, a small group of new believers who were on fire for God. They had come to their beliefs under the teaching and evangelism of an itinerant missionary from Barbados named John H. Hartman. Several times a year Rev. Hartman would travel from island to island on a small inter-island steamer to visit his various congregations in the Caribbean, including the little church that he had planted on the island of Martinique. The year 1902, though, was different.

In a journal written by Dr. V. Raymond Edman, former missionary to Ecuador, who was for many years the beloved and highly respected president of Wheaton College, we can read Rev. Hartman's own words:

"Only once did my wife, Mrs. Hartman, ever ask me not to go on one of those trips. Many a time she was ill with some tropical fever, to be sure; but only on one occasion did she beg me not to go as I had planned. I explained to her that I had no alternative but to go. The steamer went only once a month. The previous month I had sent letters to each congregation along the way to inform them that on the boat's next trip I would come for some services. The steamer remained in a given harbor for a day or two, sometimes more. Each local congregation knew approximately the day of arrival and would send word about my coming to the members and friends scattered in the towns, villages and plantations. In those days we had no wireless or radio service, and, of course, no air mail. I had to go, or else disappoint every congregation throughout the islands."

But on this one occasion, Mrs. Hartman expressed great apprehension for him. Though she was seldom discouraged, worried, or blue, she had a foreboding about this trip, scheduled for early May, 1902, and she felt that if he started out he would never return. It was such a strong impression, that Rev. Hartman reluctantly agreed to stay in Barbados.

Back on the island of Martinique, things had progressively gotten uglier. Rev. Hartman later related further to Dr. Edman: "With this mounting wickedness and depravity, there came increasingly violent persecution of the believers. They were subject to physical harm and imprisonment as well as insolence and insults from their fellow citizens, filled with strong drink and heady with sordid pleasures. Finally the persecution grew so intense that the Christians felt they could no longer remain in the city. As a result they gathered together what few belongings they could take with them and went as a group from St. Pierre. They obeyed literally the words of the Savior, 'When ye depart out of that house or city, shake off the dust of your feet… When they persecute you in this city, flee ye into another' (Matthew 10:14, 23)."

The anti God feelings on Martinique seemed to be played out even more forcefully during the Christian holiday seasons, and 1902's season of Lent and Easter saw the depravity hit new lows. The things that happened made some of the shameful things we might see today at Mardi Gras seem tame in comparison.

In fact, we read from Days and Nights in the Tropics, by Dean Harris, which was published 1905, "in parody of the Christ's journey from Pilate's house to Calvary, with a rope around its neck they dragged a living pig outside the city. Here they nailed it to a cross, lifted it on high, and with shouts and curses, apostrophized it. They hailed it as Jesus Christ, crowned its wretched head with thorns, pierced its side and put a board above it with the inscription 'J.C., King of the Christians,' and yelling and dancing like fiends, carried it through the streets.

Then, at about the same hour, another procession of human devils, ascended the mountain behind the city, uprooted a great crucifix that had stood there for many years, and amid obscene rites and blasphemous songs, cast the sacred figure into the crater, their leader yelling as it sank out of sight, 'Go where Thou deservest to go, into Thine own hell."

At the same time that these atrocities were occurring, there were two missionaries in Canada who felt a strong pull to go to Martinique as two witnesses of the Gospel. They boarded a ship and headed for the Caribbean. When their ship reached its destination, the immigration officer naturally asked them what their plans were on the island. When told that they planned to preach about Jesus, he refused their entry, making them remain on board the ship until it left the harbor. Martinique had no desire to hear the Gospel.

Early in the morning of May 8, 1902, the Canadian missionaries' ship pulled out of the harbor. As it was leaving, the steamship that should have been carrying Rev. Hartman came into port.

It was the Day of Ascension, the day of celebration held annually forty days after Easter Sunday to commemorate the ascension of Christ into heaven. What new ideas the blasphemous citizenry had for that afternoon to try to top their earlier activities during Easter we can not know. What we do know is reported to us by the people on a cable repair ship that had the city in direct view.

At exactly 7:52 that morning of the Day of Ascension, the mountain behind the city violently split in half and a dense black cloud shot out horizontally. A second black cloud rolled upwards, forming a gigantic mushroom cloud, completely darkening the sky for a fifty mile radius. The initial speed of both clouds was later calculated to be over 420 miles per hour.

According to Wikipedia: "The horizontal cloud hugged the ground and sped down towards the city of Saint-Pierre, appearing black and heavy, glowing hot from the inside. It consisted of superheated steam and volcanic gases and dust, with temperatures exceeding 1075 °C. In under a minute it reached and covered the entire city, instantly igniting everything flammable it came in contact with.

A rush of wind followed, this time towards the mountain. Then came a half-hour downpour of muddy rain mixed with ashes. For the next several hours, all communication with the city was severed. Nobody knew what was happening, nor who had authority over the island, as the governor was unreachable and his status unknown.

One eyewitness said "the mountain was blown to pieces, there was no warning", while another said "it was like a giant oil refinery". One person even went as far to say that "the town vanished before our eyes." A warship approached the shore at about 12:30, but the intense heat prevented it from landing until about 3 PM. The city burned for several more days."

The two missionaries from Canada who were turned away witnessed the unbelievable sight from miles away. The steamship Rev. Hartman was suppose to be on was totally destroyed, as was every other ship in the harbor. Only one resident in the city survived to tell the tale. The rest of the population of over 30,000 people perished, incinerated in the first few seconds, as was virtually all of the animal and bird life. The sea literally boiled for miles out from the island. The lone survivor in the city was a murderer who had been in a dungeon like jail cell under the ground. The air in his underground chamber literally roasted his skin, but he lived to relate his story.

The small Christian church watched the devastation from their new home. The ship carrying the two Canadian Christian witnesses was burning from stem to stern when it reached the next island of St. Lucia; however, the two missionaries were not injured. Fire fell from the eruption down on neighboring islands as far as 125 miles away, from the volcano that was Mt. Pelee, the mountain where the large crucifix had been tossed in six weeks earlier, with the heinous shout, "Go where Thou deservest to go, into Thine own hell."

The editor of The Dominica Guardian, on May 28, 1902, wrote, "The profanities on last Good Friday at St. Pierre were but the repetitions of similar profanities and sacrilegiousness of which we know too much. But an outraged Divinity having hushed up the actors forever we will say no more about them."

Rev. John H. Hartman and his small congregation of believers were reunited, and Martinique is today the lush paradise it was intended to be.

The questions to ponder, dear reader, are these: Does God still orchestrate events in the modern day as He did in Biblical days? And if so, does He do it in such a way as to insert shadows of future events as a form of prophecy for modern mankind to learn from? If so, what shadows could be in this, one of the most incredible stories of all time? And since we know that "shadows" in the Bible usually depict events, and a Biblical "type" normally depicts a divine or mortal person, could God have included any "types" in this modern day event?

In my research I was astounded to find that, as far as I know, no other person has ever looked at the events of the Mt. Pelee Ascension Day eruption in this light of searching for Types and Shadows. Interestingly, you and I may be the first people on earth ever to do so.

My belief is that God did not stop communicating to us with the writing of the last word in Revelation. We know that God *"is the same yesterday, today, and forever,"* and since his communication was relatively constant up until two thousand years ago, it seems to make sense that He probably did not stop then. We also know that up until today He does continue to communicate to mankind in prayer, situational direction, dreams, visions, etc. Before you jump up and down, though, please be certain that I realize that the Bible is the final word on any matter. And know also that it would be easy to go way overboard in trying to read things into every historical event. But when something seems to have God's hand so openly on it, even down to the timing being on the Day of Ascension, it might be worthwhile to explore some possibilities.

Our Father orchestrated historical events to tell us things in the shadows or pictures within the events themselves, such as those in the book of Ruth that most Christians are familiar with. Those "shadows" were a form of prophecy. The people involved had no idea that they were living out prophetic dramas, but they certainly were. We can be confident that Abraham had no idea when he was told to take his son, Isaac, up on a mountain and sacrifice him that what he was doing was a picture of God Himself having to take Jesus, His Son, up the very same mountain hundreds of years later to sacrifice Him as a substitution for sinful mankind. After 15,000 hours of research I have come to believe that virtually every event described in the Bible contains these shadows, including even the miracles of Christ, our Savior.

For instance, although I will not go into all the details now, even the two stories of the feedings of the multitudes are full of such shadows, indicating the old and new covenants. For example, the two baskets used to pick up the remaining fish were different Hebrew words, one describing a basket used exclusively by Jews, and the other describing one used by Gentiles. Reread those miracles sometime and notice how even the numbers are different. Twelve of the Jewish baskets were retrieved in one feeding, obviously representing the twelve tribes of Israel, whereas seven of the Gentile baskets were filled at the end of the other feeding, representing the seven churches, as in the seven churches Jesus wrote letters to in Revelation.

With the knowledge that God indeed orchestrated all of the Biblical events in order to tell us things, my feeling is that some events since then could, in fact, be loaded with "types and shadows" and prophecy. The story we saw that happened in Martinique in 1902 may be a prime example. As you read the accounts, you probably saw the wrath of God and Judgement Day played out in that story, but could there have been more? Although no one else in the past hundred years seems to have noticed, I for one believe there well might be much more.

God's overall story to us is a fairly simple one in many regards, and because of that, most Biblical stories contain types and shadows that portray the same themes over and over. Personally, I see many of the exact same ones in the Martinique story. You may feel that what I am going to share is a stretch, but humor me for a moment.

Below are the "types and shadows" that jumped out at me:

1 - The wrath of God and Judgement Day. That one is too obvious to discuss.

2 - Could the traditional church on the island represent the end time church that Jesus said He would spit out of His mouth in His letter to the Church of Laodicia in Revelation? As we know, that church, which is probably our church age, was said to be luke warm. It will become a completely apostate (unbelieving) church during the Tribulation according to the book of Revelation.

3 - I see the small church of on-fire believers that was *led* to leave as a shadow of the rapture. We know that God always takes His children out of the way before He shows His wrath, as was the case of Noah's family during the flood and Lot's family before the destruction of Sodom and Gamorrah. That, by the way, is just one of the many, many reasons I foresee a pre-tribulation rapture instead of a mid-tribulation or post-tribulation rapture as being the only viable timing for the rapture. As an aside, an interesting question for mid-trib or post-trib believers is, "Why would an engaged man beat up his fiancé right before the wedding feast?" Obviously he would not. And Jesus will not torture His believing church by making them go through the tribulation either. Actually, as we discussed in Unlocking God's Secrets, His bride will be attending the marriage feast in heaven at the same time the tribulation will be occurring on earth.

4 - One of the most obvious "types" in the Martinique story is that of the two Canadian men who

came to witness, but whose message was not wanted. They clearly represent the Two Witnesses in Revelation who will be sent to preach the Gospel but will be hated to the point that their killing is a time for celebration.

5 - Speaking of that small band of believers that left before the eruption in our story, could Rev. Hartman represent the Holy Spirit? He obviously was the overseer of the small church, and he was kept away during the wrath and fury. Similar "types" for the Holy Spirit are found in the Bible.

6 - The leader of the blasphemous citizens looks to me like a "type" of the Antichrist.

7 - And the defiant act that he committed with the pig was to me an obvious shadow of the "abomination that causes desolation" spoken of in places such as Daniel, Mark, Matthew, and Revelation.

8 - The actual fire itself seems extremely representative, since God tells us over and over that He will cleanse the earth of sin the second time with fire, not a flood. The heat of the fire on Martinique surpassed a thousand degrees centigrade. Everything was completely destroyed.

9 - And in mentioning the fire, notice that after the total "cleansing" on Martinique occurred, the island came back as a completely lush paradise. This to me is a "shadow" of what we are told will happen to the earth after it is cleansed by fire when the Millennial Kingdom is over, so that heaven can then be on this earth.

10 - Another "type" that springs to mind is the murderer in the dungeon who survives the devastation. I

can see him as representing Satan. At the end of the tribulation, when unbelievers are destroyed, Satan is put in a dungeon and allowed to live on until the end of the Millennial Kingdom when he is released for a short time.

11 - The mountain splitting in two is a perfect picture of what we are told will happen to the Mount of Olives on the day that Jesus will return.

12 - What about Jesus? Is there a "type" of Him in this story? I actually see Him twice. First, I think the crucifix that was thrown into the pit represented what happened to him for three days following His crucifixion. Second, I see the forceful eruption on the Day of Ascension as representing His power, which we seem to forget to think about way too much.

Virtually every story, event, parable and miracle in the Bible is rich with the symbolisms of "types and shadows" which foretell future events and people. God orchestrated things that way up until two thousand years ago in order to prophecy events that were to come. Did the Father change His way of doing things after John wrote the last word in Revelation? I don't believe He did. Hebrews 13:8 tells us, *"Jesus is the same today and yesterday and forever."* It is still His earth. It is still "His story." Those in the world today who don't take advantage of God's grace, and rush to the feet of Jesus now, will someday experience the same destruction that the citizens of Saint-Pierre, Martinique, did in 1902. God has given mankind thousands and thousands of prophecies and shadows so that man would understand the future and run to Him before it is too late. Our loving Father has even orchestrated history, His story, to try to reach the children He so dearly loves.

A Drive in the Rain

My wife and I have come up with a plan that works pretty good. When we are on a trip we swap the driving chores about every hour. That way neither of us get as many "driving" headaches and we can rest when not at the wheel. I have come to enjoy this way of traveling and have gotten into a little routine. When it's Barb's turn to drive, I recline the passenger seat, put a pillow behind my head, and often instantly doze off. Barb probably likes my routine, too, because while snoozing I am not as prone to give driving instructions like we men seem to be programmed to do.

Several years ago we were driving to Canada and it came my turn to take a nap. I didn't resist at all and was soon in dreamland. Unfortunately I was abruptly brought back to reality by a heavy pounding of a torrential downpour and the constant smashing of windshield wipers going full speed. When I opened my eyes it was apparent that I could see nothing at all outside the car. It was as if we were driving through Niagara Falls. There was absolutely no way to see the road.

Maybe with a very little touch of panic in my voice, I gently pondered out loud if it might not be wise to pull over until the lake that was cascading down on us had run its course. Barb, though, replied that there was nothing to worry about because she was following a big truck and as long as she stayed close enough to see his tail lights, which she assured me she could, all would be fine and dandy. Her confidence reassured me and I closed my eyes, thinking I would prefer to be asleep when the crash occurred than be fully awake and have to witness the obvious crushing accident that was going to occur.

To sleep I went, but some time later I was wakened again, this time to the sound of Barb saying something like, "Oh, my." Actually, I doubt that those were her exact words. At any rate, when I could focus my eyes I could see that we were coming out of the storm. What had shaken Barb was the realization that there was no truck in front of us. There was nothing in front of us at all.

At the time we were driving a Lincoln Town Car and that model had little red lights on each front fender that told the driver that the headlights were on. The "truck" Barb had been following for miles and miles during the blinding rain storm was in reality our car's own little lights on the front fenders. Nothing else was driving on the highway in that downpour of the century.

I can attest to the fact that Barb could not see any of the road in front of her as she was driving. Did God send angels to keep our car on the pavement that day? Considering the title of this book, that is something you can muse about. As for me, I will just mention something a dear friend of mine has often said when faced with questions like this, "For those who don't believe, no explanation will do. For those who believe, no explanation is needed."

Clothes Make the Man

For those of you who enjoy seeing a mystery solved, this mini study should be a treat, for we will solve one that has eluded scholars for thousands of years. Actually, we will learn the hidden secret of several unresolved Biblical mysteries. Although I could write chapters about these "shadows," I will attempt to cover them here extremely briefly. Let's first go all the way back to the story of Joseph and his master's wife, and a verse which says, *"She caught him by his cloak and said, 'Come to bed with me!' but he left his cloak in her hands and ran out of the house."* Genesis 39:12.

She then lied to her husband, telling him that Joseph had tried to seduce her, and that the cloak he left behind was the proof. As we might imagine, a few verses later we find that, *"Joseph's master took him and put him in prison, the place where the king's prisoners were confined."* Genesis 39:20.

There have been a lot of sermons preached and books written about this episode, but never have I found any mention of the deep meaning of this story. Unfortunately, it is so easy to get caught up in the surface stories of the Bible without ever looking at the deeper and more important spiritual things that I believe God truly wants us to understand. This one actually is quite simple if we just go back to the beginning where we find Adam and Eve after they ate the forbidden fruit. They realized that they were naked and tried to cover themselves with fig leaves. Their nakedness represented sin. This picture is consistent throughout God's Word.

In Joseph's case, the same is true. When Potiphar's wife was left holding his cloak, he was naked. Joseph, of course, is a "type" of Jesus. Much has been written about that. But what has escaped any that I have read or heard was that this entire story is a complete shadow of what was to happen to Jesus, for like the Savior, though sinless, Joseph was accused of sinning and thrown into the king's prison (the king being a "type" of God, and His prison representing hell). Obviously, this was what happened later to our Lord.

Let's fast forward now to one of the most seemingly out of place and mysterious passages in the Bible. When Jesus was arrested that monumental night in the garden, we read, *"Then everyone departed and fled. A young man wearing nothing but a linen garment, was following Jesus. When they seized him, he fled naked, leaving his garment behind."* Mark 14:50-51.

Quite honestly, I read that scripture countless times and I never knew what it was there for. The only time I had ever heard it mention was with the idea that the young man was Mark himself, and he was just trying to tell us that he had actually seen what had happened. That could be true. We don't know. But I still felt there must be more to it than that.

We are told that the Holy Spirit will instruct us, and I personally have come to rely on Him to do just that. With that in mind, a few months ago I asked Him to explain this scripture to me. I told Him that I wanted to know what the Father wanted us to understand about it.

A few hours later the surprising answer came. The young man was a picture of Jesus himself. The moment He was arrested, just like Joseph, He was accused of sins He did not commit. His linen cloak was stripped from Him. The fact is that He took on Himself all of my sins. He took on Himself all of your sins. He was then going to be beaten and have to die a gruesome death because of our sins. And for three days He would have to go into hell, the King's prison, as a just punishment for our sinful lives.

Yes, clothes make the man. Complete nakedness speaks of sin. A white robe, which we will receive in heaven because of our making Jesus our Lord, tells of righteousness. And a linen robe goes even one step further and expresses total holiness. In Jesus' case, His garment was linen. He was totally holy. But even more than that, we read of the soldiers casting lots for His clothes at the foot of the cross, and we read a word that God explicitly put in His description of that garment that He wanted us to pay attention to. It is spiritually even more meaningful. For we are told, *"This garment was seamless, woven in one piece from top to bottom. 'Let's not tear it,' they said to one another."* John 19:23-24.

Yes, the garment of Jesus was linen, He was holy. So holy that there was not even a stitch on His garment. It was seamless. Not one sin that He died for was His. They were all yours, and they were all mine. He was divinely holy. His linen garment was seamless, and I believe that word speaks of a holiness that is so far above what we have previously considered that it is completely unimaginable to us. Beyond that, His garment was not torn. Praise God, that is right. And once He did what had to be done for us, His garment remained the same. It was not torn. Today He sits on high, in total, unimaginable holiness, adorned in a seamless linen garment. There is none like Him. How could we possibly not worship such an awesome Savior?

But there is even more. In Mark16:5, when the women looked into the empty tomb, it says, *"they saw a young man dressed in a white robe sitting on the right side."* I believe that this man was also a picture of Jesus. Jesus had lost His righteousness in the Garden when He was arrested, because He had to be "made sin for us" and carry our sins to the cross. What the women saw in the tomb was a "shadow" of Jesus with His righteousness in tack after he was crucified, buried, arose, and did His work for our salvation. His white robe was back on.

Notice also that the "shadow" was sitting on "the right side," an allusion to Jesus sitting at the right side of the Father as King of kings. And as you may remember, Mark is the gospel that gives us the picture of Jesus' kingship.

This, to me, is an exciting revelation and puts the pieces together of the young man running away in the garden, and the young man in the tomb. They are both pictures of Jesus, showing Him without and with His righteousness. The Bible never ceases to amaze me.

Jesus the Joker

There is an episode in the life of Jesus that puts a grin on my face whenever I read it. You're probably familiar with the story. It is the one in which Jesus met a man who had been demon possessed and lived in the tombs. The man was such a mess that he lived naked and had been driven by the demons to live in solitary places. When he met Jesus he started shouting, *"What do you want with me, Jesus, Son of the Most high God? I beg you, don't torture me!' For Jesus had commanded the evil spirit to come out of the man."* Luke 8:28-29.

"Jesus asked him, 'What is your name?'

'Legion,' he replied, because many demons had gone into him. And they begged Him repeatedly not to order them into the abyss.

A large herd of pigs was feeding there on the hillside. The demons begged Jesus to let them go into them, and He gave them permission. When the demons came out of the man, they went into the pigs, and the herd rushed down the steep bank into the lake and was drowned." Luke 8:30-33.

So, why does that make me grin? Is it because Jesus played a joke on the demons? Kind of, but it is funnier than just that. Think for a moment with me. Obviously those pigs were in no way used by Jews. Pigs were disgusting in the Jewish culture. They would never eat them. They had no use for them. So, what were those pigs there for?

This is where searching out the matter can result in fun and surprises. The fact is that Jesus was in the region of the Gerasenes. This was not Jewish countryside. The people in that region worshiped idols made of wood and stone. And the way they worshiped these worthless gods was to sacrifice pigs to the idols. Yes, Jesus sent the demons into the lake, but at the same time He destroyed months and maybe years of pig production that was meant for the sacrifices to false gods. If it had been possible, I suppose some stone idols had pouty faces for a long time to come.

I'll bet Jesus had a grin on His face when He went to sleep that night. Talk about a practical joke! That one ranks as one of the best of all time.

Two Men

By now you probably understand how fascinated I am with "Types and Shadows" in the Bible. There are thousands of them and quite literally they tell the same story as the surface writing does. It is extremely intriguing to see how intricately God told His story just below the surface of his Word. It proves conclusively to me that only a divine being like God could have written the Bible.

Today we will look at a sampling of one that runs throughout the entire scriptures. I call it the "two men" shadow.

As we discussed in the last article, Joseph is a "type" of Jesus. There are so many similarities between the two that it is uncanny. Let's look at the story about Joseph in prison with the two men who had dreams. One was a cupbearer to Pharaoh, and the other was his chief baker. You can read the story of their dreams and Joseph's interpretations in Genesis 40. I'll just skip to the chase and say that the cupbearer was restored to his position and the chief baker was killed.

Like me, you may have read this account several times without seeing the hidden shadow. Once you see it, though, it will be as clear as one of those fuzzy pictures you stare at for a few minutes that then become a clear picture. Those two men represent the two thieves on the cross. They are a shadow of what was to come on Golgotha. One thief got to be in paradise with Jesus. The other did not. As I said, the entire story of Joseph is the story of Jesus.

Shadows, however, often carry on beyond what we think to be the fulfillment. In this case, the types of the two men with Joseph come to fruition with the two thieves on the cross, but the shadow continues. Those two thieves also represent you and me. We can either accept Jesus as Lord of our lives and enter paradise, or we can choose not to, and enter destruction. There is not a third position for us to take.

We all know that Jesus said in John 14:6, *"I am the way and the truth and the life. No one comes to the Father except through me."* But have we also paid attention to His profound statement in Luke 11:23, *"He who is not with me is against me, and he who does not gather with me, scatters."*

Are you gathering with Jesus?

The Love that Matters

There is a verse that causes many Christians to flinch. In it Jesus tells us, *"If anyone comes to Me, and does not hate his father and mother, his wife and children, his brothers and sisters, yes, even his own life, he cannot be My disciple."* Luke 14:26

Wow! Is Jesus really telling us to hate everybody in our family? Obviously there must be a mistake. And quite frankly, there is. The problem lies in the translation of the Greek word, "miseo," into our English word, "hate." Yes, "miseo" can mean "hate," but it also has another meaning, which is "to love less by comparison." The latter meaning is what Jesus unquestionably meant. I suppose the translators were going through some economic troubles like we are today and felt that it would be prudent to try to save some ink, but in the process they succeeded only in causing some difficulties.

But knowing the correct translation should still make some of us flinch. Do we, in fact, love Jesus more than any of our other loved ones? Jesus says that unless we do we can not be one of His disciples. He did not say we might not. He said we can not.

We must remember that Jesus told us in Matthew 22:37 that the most important commandment is, *"You shall love the Lord your God with all your heart and with all your soul and with all your mind."* Jesus did not suggest this. He commanded it. And He was repeating a commandment given in Deuteronomy 6:5. This is the number one commandment, above all others, and it may be the one that is broken by more people than any other. In fact, it is seldom even thought about.

We would not even think of committing murder because we know that is breaking a commandment. We do not steal for the same reason. But the most important commandment is shattered to pieces continually by people who call themselves Christians.

The answer is simple to state: build a relationship with Jesus and the Father through time spent in prayer and in God's Word, and the loving part always follows. It always does.

"But, Bob, I work all day. Come home and eat. Spend a few hours in front of the TV. And crash. There is no time for Bible study and relationship building prayer every day."

Then ponder this. We may need to consider that the question at this point may not be whether we love Jesus more than our family. The question may be even more basic than that. Do we even love Jesus more than a "Law and Order" rerun or the "American Idol" program or the evening news. Personally, I would not want that pointed out to me by our Lord on the day my spirit leaves this earthly body.

The entire history of mankind has been about one thing, and one thing only, and that is to find a bride for Christ. Everything else in world history, and in our individual lives, is so incredibly incidental as to be totally meaningless. And as with every marriage, a deeply loving relationship is the key. Our real future, the long term eternal one, is our choice. This earthly life is not a game.

"Wide is the gate and broad is the road that leads to destruction, and many enter through it. But small is the gate and narrow the road that leads to life, and only a few find it."
Spoken by Jesus Himself in Matthew 7:13-14.

Humor in Esther

A few pages back we saw how Jesus was a practical joker when He sent the demons into the pigs and they ran into the lake and were drowned. When we "searched out the matter" we found that the biggest part of the joke was that the pigs were being raised to be used as sacrifices to idols. The deeper we dig into the scriptures the more we find that God truly does have a sense of humor. My favorite example is found in the book of Esther.

On the surface, Esther is one of the strangest books in the Bible. I say that because nowhere in the entire book is God even mentioned. In fact, arguments raged for years with people saying that Esther should be eliminated from God's Word. Of course, God's will prevailed and Esther is now a permanent part of the Bible. Since we are becoming aware of the intricacies of the "shadows" that God placed in His scriptures, we can understand now why that book is so important to Him. Read the book with an eye for "types and shadows" and you will see that they abound. The most obvious is that Haman, the evil person who wants to destroy God's children in the story, is actually a "type" of Satan.

You may recall that in chapter 3, verse 9, Haman says to the King, *"If it pleases the king, let a decree be issued to destroy them* (The Jews)*, and I will put ten thousand talents of silver into the treasury for the men who carry out this business."*

Verses 10 and 11 continue, *"So the king took his*

50

signet ring and gave it to Haman son of Hammedatha, the Agite, the enemy of the Jews. 'Keep the money,' the king said to Haman, 'and do with the people as you please.'

It is here that I laugh out loud. The reason is the coding underneath the surface words. As you may know, high speed computers are now finding sentences, and even complete paragraphs, hidden under the surface text in *equidistant letter sequence* codes, or ELS in decoders' parlance. That just means that words are spelled out by looking at the original Hebrew text and skipping letters by a certain number. Under the above verses 10 and 11, by counting every 6th letter ten times (think of 666), we find a phrase that cracks me up. And only someone as super intelligent as our God could create such an amazing book as the Bible with these hidden and coded messages throughout.

The phrase God hid for those of us lucky enough to be alive at this period of high speed computers is truly a gem, for under the above scriptures about Haman wanting to kill all the Jews, spaced in six letter intervals, God wrote, "Haman and Satan stink."

Water Into Wine

Let's look at another incredible "shadow" that to my knowledge has never been written or talked about before. As you know, I believe firmly that the more we "search out the matter" of shadows, the more we find just how phenomenal God's Word truly is. They prove unquestionably that no human mind could have ever come close to writing the intricacy that is our Bible.

Most of us understand that God used days throughout His Word as shadows of thousand year periods, primarily as predictors of the time of Christ's second coming. For instance, the six days of work and one of rest in the creation story signifies the six thousand years before the thousand year millennial reign of Jesus, the same as does the scripture in Hosea 6:2 in which we read, *"After two days he will revive us; on the third day he will restore us, that we may live in his presence."* Those two days, of course, refer to the two thousand year period from Christ's ascension after He arose until His second coming; as do the two days mentioned in Exodus 19:10-11 which says, *"Go to the people and consecrate them today and tomorrow. Have them wash their clothes and be ready by the third day, because on that day the Lord will come down on Mount Sinai in the sight of the people."*

Unfortunately, it seems that the relatively few scholars who do pay close attention to Biblical shadows normally quit looking beyond the Old Testament. What a shame that is, because shadows in the New Testament in my opinion are just as plentiful. In fact, my personal belief is that if we spend enough time in study and prayer about it we will find that every miracle and parable of Jesus is a shadow that will give us prophecy of things yet to come. For example, in the New Testament the beginning of the passage that talks about the transfiguration of Jesus into glory personified on the mountain top is almost always overlooked, although it starts out with the telling phrase, *"After six days ..."* Matthew 17:1. Again, that is a shadow prophesying that Jesus will come in his glory after the six thousand years from the beginning of Biblical recording.

The brand new shadow I want to share with you today is found in the very first miracle of Jesus, the changing of water into wine. How often the story is retold and written about, but no one ever looks beyond the obvious. Yes, the miracle itself is exciting, but the story God has hidden within it in the form of shadows is even more so. For brevity sake, we will look at only a few of the shadows in this astounding and intricately encoded story.

Although you may have read this story a hundred times, you probably never noticed before that it begins in John 2:1 with, *"On the third day ..."* Wow! I know that I was amazed how many times I overlooked it before I opened my eyes to the spiritual things God has for us in His unbelievably wonderful Word.

OK, so now that we are alert, let's read a little more. *"On the third day a wedding took place."* Wow, again. Now it makes sense. Yes, we know the wedding feast of the Lamb will occur in heaven after the two thousand years following Christ's ascension, but before His second coming. *"On the third day."*

John 2:6 tells us, *"Nearby stood six stone water jars, the kind used by the Jews for ceremonial washing ..."* Remember, every word in the Bible is there for a reason. My personal feeling is that God is referring to the six thousand years the Jews have had a religion of ceremonies; not a relationship with His precious Holy Spirit. Of course, you know the miracle. With the water in those jars, Jesus made wine. And wine always represents that loving Holy Spirit. *"On the third day .."* the Jews will be united with the Spirit of God. Jesus will turn ceremony into relationship for the Jewish nation, the apple of God's eye.

The fabulous story ends in verse 11 with, *"He thus revealed His glory ..."* This is the same glory revealed in Jesus on that Mountain of Transfiguration. And it is the same glory you and I will see in person *"on the third day."*

Only God could have written our Bible. What a treasure of golden nuggets it is!

Our Two Days

In the last pages we explored just a few of the instances in the Bible in which God used two days in shadows to represent two thousand years. Of course, the major clue for interpreting these hidden nuggets is found in 2 Peter 3:8, where we read, *"With the Lord a day is like a thousand years and a thousand years are like a day."*

Normally references to "two days" or the "third day" refer to Christ's second coming to save His chosen nation, Israel. The New Testament is full of such pictures, such as in the story of Jesus raising the Hebrew, Lazarus, from the dead. The Bible says, *"Yet when He heard that Lazarus was sick, he stayed where He was **two more days**."* John 11:6. Like most people, you may not have noticed that phrase before, but the more we get attuned to shadows in the Bible, the more we realize that God is showing us that Jesus will stay in heaven for two thousand years before He returns to earth to redeem the Hebrew people, exactly as God had promised the patriarchs, Abraham, Isaac, and Jacob. Of course the granddaddy of all of these "third day" pictures is the death and resurrection of Christ. Not only is that time period given to us in the Gospels, but also in places like Acts 10:40, *"God raised him from the dead on the **third day** and caused Him to be seen."*

But what about us Gentiles? What about the church, the bride of Christ? Does God give us the same assurance in a two day shadow form as he does Israel? The answer is yes, but once again I have never seen it written about or any sermon preached on it. It is as if our scholars have never noticed it before. Once again, what a shame. The shadow I am referring to is found in the story of the Samaritan woman at the well in John 4.

We all know the story. In fact you may have read it dozens of times. But were your spiritual eyes open? Mine weren't for probably the first hundred times that I read it. It seems that God opens our eyes when He is ready for us to see what he has hidden within the scriptures.

Before we look at this fantastic shadow, let's first be clear that the Samaritans were not Jews. They were Gentiles. And the story of the Samaritan woman and her fellow townspeople is one of the very few accounts of Jesus dealing with anyone other than His fellow Jews. We might get a clue from that fact that this story is one directed to us, and as we shall see, it is. We'll take up the story after Jesus told the woman about her past husbands and then responded to her statement about the coming Messiah by saying to her, *"I who speak to you am he."*

We then learn, *"Many of the Samaritans from the town believed in Him because of the woman's testimony, 'He told me everything I ever did.' So when the Samaritans came to Him, they urged Him to stay with them, and He stayed* **two days**. *And because of His words many more became believers. They said to the woman, 'We no longer believe just because of what you said; now we have heard for ourselves, and we know that this man really is the Savior of the world."* John 4:39-42.

There actually are several shadows in that short

story, but let's concentrate on the "two days." Anytime God uses the two days in reference to the Jews, He always is seen as waiting for that time period to pass before He acts, such as the case with Lazarus. In the case of the Samaritans, who represent us, though, Christ stays with them for the two days. That, of course has been the case. Jesus has stayed with us, His Gentile Church, in the form of the Holy Spirit. And He has stayed with us for "two days."

In regards to the Jews, their eyes have been blinded for the past two thousand years. John 12:40 says, *"He has blinded their eyes and deadened their hearts, so they can neither see with their eyes, nor understand with their hearts, nor turn and I would heal them."* This was done so that we Gentiles would have time to come to Him, and the past two thousand years is referred to in Luke 21:24 as *"The time of the Gentiles."*

Yes, Jesus has given us a chance for eternal life, and has even stayed with us in the person of the precious Holy Spirit for these past two thousand years, but the time is quickly drawing to a close. If the "two days" are counted in Jewish years, their end was 2005. If God is counting them in "Gentile" years, the two days is up 2032. Either way, and with countless other clues within God's Word, we can know for a certainty that it is about time for the rapture of Christ's Gentile Church, which will usher in the last seven years of tribulation designed to open their eyes and bring in His beloved Jewish nation.

Ride of a Life

What a wonderful day it was. Roger Simms had finished his stint in the army that morning and was on his way to begin his new life. His uniform had been happily exchanged for some civies, and Roger was on the road home, thumb outstretched, daydreaming about what might lie ahead for him in his future.

After a fairly short wait a beautiful new car pulled up, driven by a distinguished gentleman who obviously had done well in his lifetime. Roger slid into the posh seat and was greeted by a warm smile that let him know the trip ahead would be a pleasant one. On top of that, in short order it was discovered that both men were heading for Chicago. Roger was heading home for the first time in years, and Mr. Hanover had both his home and his business there as well.

Although Roger was a Christian, what came next was a complete surprise to him. An inexplicable urge came over him to talk to Mr. Hanover about Jesus. There had been times in years past when Roger felt that he should probably witness to someone or other, but nothing like this strange tugging urge had ever occurred.

The miles rolled on, and although Mr. Hanover was an extremely interesting conversationalist on several topics, Roger had a difficult time concentrating on what was being said for the overwhelming thought that to say nothing about Christ was not an option for him. Finally, Roger timidly obeyed, "Mr. Hanover, I think I should talk to you about something important." And he went on, explaining the plan of salvation without a comment or even a nod from the then stone faced businessman. At the end of what seemed like an eternity to Roger, he asked Mr. Hanover if he would like to receive Jesus as his Savior.

The big car pulled to the side of the road and Roger felt that his luxury ride was over. But instead of being asked to step out, Mr. Hanover bowed his head, crying, and saying yes, he did want Christ to save him. The drive from that moment on was one of complete joy for both men, two new brothers in Christ Jesus.

Mr. Hanover drove Roger right to his parents' front door in a southern suburb of Chicago, and the men shook hands and hugged, both knowing that the ride they had just completed was a trip orchestrated by God Himself. Neither would ever forget that special May 7th.

Five years passed. Roger Simms got married and the couple had a beautiful child, the apple of Roger's eye. Roger also started a little business for himself and things seemed to be going pretty good. One day he needed to go to downtown Chicago on business and he decided to carry along with him the embossed card that Mr. Hanover had given him as they parted ways on that special day five years earlier.

Roger found the address on the card to be a very impressive high rise office building in the heart of the business district. The receptionist at Hanover Enterprises said that it was impossible to see Mr. Hanover, but that if he wished, Roger could meet with Mrs. Hanover since he evidently was an old friend. Disappointed, he agreed.

Sitting behind an impressive oak desk sat an attractive woman in her mid fifties who extended her hand, saying, "I take it you knew my husband. You may not know that he passed away."

Roger explained how her husband had been kind enough to give him a ride home some years earlier.

"Do you happen to know when that was?" Mrs. Hanover asked.

"Sure, it was the day I was discharged from the army, May 7th, five years ago."

"And did anything special happen that day ... anything unusual?" Mrs. Hanover continued.

This line of questioning seemed a little awkward. Roger wondered if what had happened that day had possibly caused some problems in their marriage, maybe even causing a separation. But Roger decided to be truthful. "Your husband prayed the prayer of salvation that day."

The dam broke. Mrs. Hanover began to sob uncontrollably. Finally, "I grew up in a Christian home, but my husband did not. He would not even talk with me about it. So I prayed, every day I prayed for him, for years I prayed. I believed God would answer my prayer. That very day, May 7th, he never made it home. Evidently the accident occurred after he dropped you off. They say he was killed instantly. Five years ago I stopped living for the Lord because I felt He had betrayed me, letting the person I loved the most in this world die without being saved."

Treasure in John

There are times when I'll look down at my Bible in utter amazement at the pure genius that went into the creation of it. We'll hear about how intricately woven the human body is, but it is possible that the Creator was just as careful in the creation of His Word. It may well be the most complex of all His masterpieces, yet sadly the world as a whole has no clue.

For instance, from the beginning to the end of both Testaments, Jesus is depicted in His four distinct characters: servant, king, man and God. The Holy Spirit intricately wove those four throughout the Bible in all sorts of ways, including the "types" of ox, lion, face of man, and eagle.

God also, of course, methodically used numbers throughout His Word to emphasize things, create shadows, and even tell complete stories. We can study the meaning that God gave to each number, such as the number five representing God's grace, six meaning man, seven standing for perfection and divinity, and eight being the number for Christ Himself. But sometimes God pointed out things numerically without even using the actual numbers. These fascinating gems were hidden from all but those willing to spend the time digging for them. And what treasures they are when brought to light.

One such case can be found in the book of John. It is fairly common knowledge that the four Gospels interestingly depict Jesus from the four different angles spoken of above. Matthew concentrates on the humanity of Jesus. Mark emphasizes His kingship. Luke points to the servant nature of Christ. And John's Gospel brings home the fact that Jesus is God.

When looking at John we might expect to see the actual number seven used abundantly, since seven represents divinity or perfection and the Gospel of John is emphasizing that part of Jesus. Quite frankly, though, that is not the case. But by digging deeper, the genius of God's masterpiece becomes even more apparent. For instance, let's look at the miracles John relates. There is the turning of water into wine, the healing of the man's son, the healing of the man at the pool, the feeding of the five thousand, Jesus walking on water, His healing of the blind man, and the climactic miracle of the raising of the dead Lazarus.

Or maybe we should study the "I am" statements made by Jesus Himself. In the book of John, Jesus told us: I am living bread, I am the light of the world, I am the good shepherd, I am the gate of the sheepfold, I am the resurrection, I am the way the truth and the life, and I am the vine.

Yes, the book of John is the depiction of Jesus as God; total perfection and completely divine. Count them yourself. There are seven miracles. And there are seven "I am" statements.

The Bible, God's Word, is the most perfect creation in all the world. Cherish it. Read it. Study it. Dig into it. And give it the reverence and awe it truly deserves. It was intricately and delicately woven specifically for you, because your Father incomparably loves you very much.

Thomas, the Man's Man

It is high time that someone stood up for a person who may be the most falsely maligned individual in all of history. For two thousand years people have ridiculed him and besmirched his good name. In fact, seldom is he ever recalled at all without people adding the insult of calling him Doubting Thomas. Today I am here to speak up for this constantly slandered soul. I now proclaim that Thomas, also known as Didymus, may well be the most honorable of all the disciples that were hand picked by the Master.

I know that other than Judas Iscariot, Thomas is the only one of the twelve looked down on by the world. But the world has bought into a lie. Yes, he had an incident we consider to be beneath a true follower of Jesus, because he was said to have doubted, but consider the facts. The Lord Himself had instructed His inner circle not to be taken in by false christs. In fact, our Savior had told them plainly, *"If anyone says to you, 'Look, here is the Christ!' or 'There he is!' do not believe it."* Matthew 24;24. So Thomas was just obeying his Teacher.

And which of us did not require convincing before we accepted the truth. Maybe it was at our mother's knee that we made the decision, but it was because she convinced us. And if we were adults when we were born again, I am sure you will agree that we didn't decide willy nilly. Jesus wanted our belief to be sure so that it would be steadfast. Yes, Thomas wanted proof, just as we did, but more importantly, because Jesus had told him to demand it.

But what kind of man was this Thomas. I submit that he was the most courageous of the bunch. Decide for yourself what kind of man he was. At one point Jesus had announced that He was going to raise Lazarus, in the area where the mobs were looking for Him to kill Him. The other eleven warned Jesus not to go by saying, *"But Rabbi, a short while ago the Jews tried to stone you, and yet you are going back there?"* John 11:8.

"Then Thomas said to the rest of the disciples, 'Let us also go, that we may die with Him." John 11:16. To me, Thomas, above all the rest, had guts. Give Peter and John all the accolades you will, but when it came crunch time, Thomas was the type of man you would want by your side. Yes, Thomas was a man's man.

` And on that day when Jesus came back to show Himself to Thomas, did Thomas hesitate? Not for a second. He saw the wounds. He instantly knew for sure it was the real Jesus and not an impostor that the Lord had warned him about, and immediately he said words that to this day send chills down my spine. Thomas fell to his knees and said, *"My Lord and my God!"* John 20:28.

After the most noble of them all uttered those haunting words, did Thomas ever once flinch from what his Master had asked of him? Not on your life. Thomas headed out and served our Lord Jesus by steadfastly preaching about our Savior in what is now Iran, Iraq, and India. He must have worn out several pairs of sandals trying to save as many people he could from eternal destruction.

Thomas was devoted beyond what any could hope for who today so self righteously malign him and think of him only as a doubter. And in the end Thomas remained loyal and noble. You see, this object of our scorn died a gruesome death, loving and serving his friend, his Master, and his Lord. The non believers in Madras, India, set him on fire trying to get him to deny Jesus. When, in excruciating pain, he would not budge on his story, they finally and mercifully put him to death by spearing him with a javelin.

How many who scoff are equal to that task? How many who unthinkably disparage him are worthy to untie his now blood soaked sandals? I can just imagine this hero of a man, as his charred and agonizing body was being run through with that spear. I can see him look up with adoration and utter through his pain, "I am yours, *'My Lord and my God."*

Doubting Thomas, my foot! We should all give this giant of courage, obedience, and honor, the highest respect possible, beyond virtually any human who ever lived. To me, Thomas is a hero among heroes. Doubting Thomas, my foot. This was a true man's man.

One Person

Here is one person's true story that should be told today. In the 1850's America was in pretty bad shape. An average guy that you have probably never heard of by the name of Jeremiah Lanphier of New York City had a simple thought. He decided to start a little noontime prayer meeting. The first one was held at the Old Dutch Church on Fulton Street on an average day, September 23, 1857. For a while Jeremiah prayed alone. Then one man came in. Finally a few more joined the duo.

The next week twenty showed up. The third week the number grew to forty. Then some other churches joined in. It then spread to other cities. Then offices and stores started closing at noon for prayer. Newspapers started writing about it. A revival broke out across America which lasted two years and is now called "The Third Great Awakening."

Between 500,000 and 1,000,000 people were saved. All because of one average Joe calling a little prayer meeting.

I can't say for sure, but I suspect that some of those new converts may have ultimately been responsible for the ending of slavery a few years later. All because of one person, surrendered to God, who prayed. Could one of us be a Jeremiah Lanphier? We will never know what God can do with any of us until we too surrender and pray.

New Knowledge

When Gabriel finished telling Daniel about the things that were to come, he instructed him in Daniel 12:4, *"But thou, O Daniel, shut up the words, and seal the book, even to the time of the end; many shall run to and fro, and knowledge shall be increased."* The truth, of course, is that knowledge today is increasing faster than imaginable, but the knowledge I think Gabriel was referring to was the knowledge of the masterful Word of God. That, too, is increasing so fast it is difficult to keep up with it. For instance, only in these past few years have we learned that the very first phrase in the first verse in the Bible actually introduced our Savior, Jesus.

As everyone knows, the first verse in Genesis says, *"In the beginning God created the heavens and the earth."* The first phrase, "in the beginning," is the Hebrew word, b'raisheet. Only recently has mankind been given the knowledge that if we start with the first yod that makes up that Hebrew word, we find in code, underneath the surface text, in an equidistant letter sequence or ELS, the Hebrew words "Yeshua yankol," which means "Jesus is the power." Wow! In the very first Hebrew word in the Bible God had already laid out the entire Bible, and only those of us who are alive today can have that knowledge. I may sound like a broken record, but there is nothing on earth as incredible as the Word of God.

But let's dig deeper. In the first four chapters we learn of the first three instances in which blood was shed.

The first time was when God went into Adam's side and extracted a rib with which to create Adam's bride. Have you ever considered that this was a picture of Jesus having His side pierced on the cross in order to bring forth His bride, the church of those who believe and are born again? When we search into the original Hebrew for Genesis 2:20, which says at the beginning of this account, *"But for Adam no suitable helper was found,"* we find that by starting with the letter mem in Adam's name there is another ELS. This one spells out "Mashiach," the Hebrew word for Messiah.

We are amazed even more when we look at the original Hebrew words in Genesis 2:22 which say, *"And the rib, which the Lord God had taken from the man, made he a woman, and brought her unto man."* In the first place, the Hebrew word for "brought", "y'vi'ehah," is the same word which is used when a father gives his daughter away in marriage. Not only that, but only today do we know also that the first lamed letter in the next verse begins another ELS that spells "l'Yeshua," which means "for Jesus." Incredibly, we also find that underneath the word "tar'daimah," the Hebrew word for the "deep sleep" in which God put Adam when he performed the operation, there is another ELS starting with the mem that once again spells "Mashiach," or Messiah.

The next shedding of blood occurs when God kills an animal, which I think was a lamb, and makes clothing to cover Adam and Eve after they realized that they were naked. This is related to us in Chapter 3:20-21. God wants us to now know for certain that this was a picture or shadow of the work Christ did on the cross. We now can be sure of that because starting with the last yod in verse 20 and counting nine letters (ELS) three times from left to right is written an astounding hidden word, "Adonai," which means "Lord." And starting with the last heh in that verse and counting nine letters (ELS) five times from right to left is the incredible word, "Yoshiah," which means "He will save."

The last instance we will look at that entailed the shedding of blood was the killing of Abel by his brother Cain. After that event we read in chapter 4:9-10, *"Then the Lord said to Cain, 'Where is your brother Abel?' 'I don't know,' he replied, 'Am I my brother's keeper?' The Lord said, 'What have you done? Listen! your brother's blood cries out to me from the ground."* This again is a shadow of what was to happen to Jesus, for He, too, was killed by His brothers. And once again God wants us to understand this shadow, because when we count every seventh letter (ELS) from left to right starting with the mem in the word for blood, "d'mai," we read "Mashiach em'met," which is the Hebrew spelling for "Messiah the Truth."

How privileged we are. Our parents did not know any of the information that you have read in the last five minutes. But this knowledge has not been given to us just so that we can be amazed and say "Wow!" Yes, it was given to us partially to increase our faith, but the main reason was so that we can use it to save others from eternal destruction. We now have this knowledge so that our friends and loved ones can be saved for a glorious eternal life with Jesus.

The greatest sin man can commit against his fellow man is to know the truth about Jesus and not tell others.

Some Mysteries Solved

I can't tell you how often I have been asked why in the world there would be the need for blood sacrifices in the Millennial Kingdom. We know that God's Word tells us that they will occur in Ezekiel 40:38-43. But Why? We know that Jesus was the fulfillment of the shadow of the Old Testament sacrifices. Hebrews 10 is very explicit about that. So why would sacrifices be necessary again when Jesus is back on earth reigning as King of kings? It just doesn't make sense.

The common thought by Biblical scholars has always been that it must be some sort of remembrance ceremony, much like communion is today. But is that the case?

In order to explain, let me take you to another New Testament mystery. John 12:20-23 says, *"Now there were some Greeks among those who went up to worship at the feast. They came to Phillip with a request, 'Sir,' they said, 'we would like to see Jesus.' Phillip went to tell Andrew; Andrew and Phillip in turn told Jesus. Jesus replied, 'the hour has come for the Son of Man to be glorified.'"* Jesus then expounds about His upcoming death.

Does that make any sense to you? It never did for me, no matter how many times I read it. Jesus never once acted in that verse like He had even heard that some Greeks wanted to see Him. In fact, it seems that the part about the Greeks coming and wanting to see Him had nothing at all to do with what came before or after it in that chapter. I normally read it, shook my head, and went on with my reading. The Greeks seeking Jesus appeared to me to not be related to anything, and I often wondered what in the world it was included for.

Finally, I stopped and asked the Holy Spirit to explain it. Unfortunately, He didn't. I read it again the next night. Still no answer. So I read it again the third night. Instantly that third night I *knew* what it was all about. And what I am going to share with you is very deep, very profound, and destined to be controversial. But let's go back to another story before I share that revelation.

Interestingly, the Canaanite woman in Matthew 15 who only wanted her daughter healed was treated miserably by Jesus. When she asked for help, Jesus said, *"It is not right to take the children's bread and toss it to their dogs."* What a way to treat this poor woman who had done nothing wrong but be a gentile. Fortunately she used logic by responding that *"Even the dogs eat the crumbs that fall from their master's table."*

Up until that point Jesus seemed to have no interest in helping her because she was not Jewish. We know that Jesus was fully divine, but mysteriously, He was also fully human. And it seems that His human side did not understand the saving of the gentiles at the beginning of His ministry. Of course, we do wonder how that could be, but that is the way Jesus is presented in scripture. The Canaanite woman's remark may have been the turning point in His human thinking.

Yes, Jesus was both fully human and fully divine. Did the Father shock the human side of Jesus into having to "search out the matter" when he presented the Son with the logic that came from the mouth of that woman? I think so. And I believe that it was between the episode with the Canaanite woman and the instance when the Greeks appeared that Jesus came to a complete understanding from studying Isaiah that no matter how long he stayed on earth, the Jews as a whole would not respond. In fact, in the same chapter where we read about the Greeks seeking Jesus, we are reminded that Isaiah 6:9 had said that the Jews would *"be ever hearing, but never understanding; be ever seeing but never perceiving."*

Up to the story of the Greeks asking to see Jesus, we know that Jesus had continued to say that His hour had not yet come. The third night after asking for the Holy Spirit's help I immediately had a brand new understanding: the cue for Jesus for the hour having arrived was the seeking of Him by the Gentiles.

What I believe could be so controversial is that I now think that the crucifixion and resurrection was never even remotely intended by the Father to be for the salvation of the Jews as a whole. The Father's plan for their salvation was all along to be manifested during the Tribulation and the Millennial Kingdom. The first coming of Christ seems to have been solely for the church.

This gives me more understanding about the other question that always comes up about the sacrifices during the Millennial Kingdom. From what I now see, the Jews were not saved at Galgotha, except of course for the Jews who have accepted the gift of salvation from Christ in the past two thousand years, and those who will make that decision before He returns.

As for the non believing Jews, could their salvation yet be achieved through some manner during the Millennial Kingdom, and could it in some way continue to entail sacrifices? Yes, Romans 11:26 teaches us, *"all Israel will be saved,"* but since we know that sacrifices will still play a big part during the Millennial Kingdom, and if the crucifixion was only for the Gentile and Messianic Jewish church, the salvation of the rest of the Jews may still hinge on their obedience to the Old Covenant during that thousand years.

The mysteries of the sacrifices during the Millennial Reign and the verse concerning the Gentile woman who was treated so poorly by Jesus and the verse about Him not seeming to pay attention to the Greeks who wanted to see Him have now been somewhat cleared up for me. As to how salvation will be accomplished for the Jews in the next thousand year period is still a mystery to me. I know that it will happen. God's Word says it will. But there are still some fuzzy areas. As the title of this book says, I suppose this is a musing, something for us to ponder and meditate on.

Prayer?

I imagine that you, like me, have wondered on occasion why you should pray? Since God is all powerful, all knowing, all loving, and totally sovereign, why does He need our prayers? Why doesn't He just take care of situations without us asking Him in prayer? Surely He could step in and take care of anything, so why doesn't He?

In <u>Unlocking God's Secrets</u> we discussed a theory put forth by Dr. Miles Monroe, a wonderful Bahamian minister. He has given us a point to ponder, or muse if you will. In Genesis 1:26, as He was creating man, God said, *"Let **them** have dominion...over all the earth"*. By saying that, God established a law, and God's law, His word, can not be broken. The **"them"** was **man**, the only spirit being in a dirt body. This law ruled out spirits without dirt bodies having dominion over the earth. Were it not so, Satan would literally have the authority to completely destroy mankind, and he probably would. He can't, though, because he doesn't have the legal right according to God's law to do so.

But ponder this, God also is spirit, and God does not break His own laws. In talking about God in Psalm 138:2, we read, *"You have magnified Your word above all Your name."* God does not put Himself above His own law, which is His word. Therefore, Dr. Monroe's thought is that God also does not have legal authority to act on this planet earth without man giving Him permission.

But, we might say, God is still sovereign. Very true, but consider this; not once since God created that law, in all of the Bible, did God act without man being involved in some way.

According to Dr. Monroe, God needs our prayers in order to have permission to legally act on this planet earth. That is why we should *"pray continually,"* as we are instructed in 1 Thessalonians 5:17. If we want God involved in our situations, and those of our loved ones, we need to pray. In order not to break His own law, God needs our permission and authority to act. We have been given dominion over all the earth. That law is still in effect. So *"pray continually."* Pray about everything. Give Him authority to act in every aspect of your life.

On a further thought, it occurs to me that our doubts cancel our prayers, as we are told in James 1:6-7, *"he who doubts ... should not think he will receive anything from the Lord."* Could that be because doubts cancel our permission for God to act? We pray, giving God permission to act, then we doubt, taking that permission away. So pray in faith, knowing that Jesus told us in Matthew 21:21, *"If you believe, you will receive whatever you ask for in prayer."*

Yes, God is all powerful, all knowing, and all loving, and by sovereignly deciding to obey the law He Himself decreed, He has declared that if we want His help, we must call on Him. His phone number is Jeremiah 33:3, *"Call on me and I will answer you"*. There is no charge for the call, so make it often.

The Days of Time

It is almost common knowledge that days in the Bible represent thousand year periods, so it might be helpful to look, with that in mind, at an overview of God's time line for man. This entire concept of changing millenniums into days in the Bible was started very early in God's Word with the relating in Genesis that God created the world in six days and rested on the seventh, and this time line is carried throughout the scriptures.

In Biblical time there were four thousand years, or four days, from Adam to Jesus. Then there are projected to be two thousand years, or two days, from the first coming of Jesus until His second coming at the end of the tribulation. This is the time period designated for the creation of Christ's true church. Following that will be the thousand year reign of Jesus, known as the Millennial Reign. In scripture, this again encompasses one day in many shadows. Finally, we read in 1 Corinthians 15:24-25, *"Then the end will come, when He* (Jesus) *hands over the kingdom to God the Father after He has destroyed all dominion, authority and power. For He must reign until he has put all His enemies under His feet. The last enemy to be defeated is death."* This final time period we can look at as the true eternal heaven, and we will see it momentarily in a shadow of the eighth day.

There are literally scores and scores of "day shadows" pertaining to each of these time periods, but let's just look at one for each one of the four time periods.

The first one, of course, is the Biblical time from Adam to Jesus. To illustrate a shadow of that, I want to look at one that I did not even notice until recently. The story is in Acts 10. A Gentile, Cornelius, who represents the Gentile church sends servants to find Peter. When Peter arrives he asks Cornelius why he had sent for him. Verses 30 to 32 tell us, *"Cornelius answered, **'Four days** ago I was in my house praying ... Suddenly a man in shining clothes stood before me and said, "Cornelius, God has heard your prayers and remembered your gifts to the poor. Send to Joppa for Simon who is called Peter."* Cornelius and his Gentile friends and family, of course, then heard from Peter the good news about Jesus and were saved. Notice that this happened after four days, a shadow of the first four thousand years on God's time table until the first coming of Jesus.

Concerning the next two thousand years, or two days, the Bible tells us that the Jews eyes were blinded. We can find that in John 12:40, *"He has blinded their eyes and deadened their hearts, so they can neither see with their eyes, nor understand with their hearts, nor turn and I would heal them."* This was done so that we Gentiles would have time to come to Him, and the past two thousand years is referred to in Luke 21:24 as *"The time of the Gentiles."* We also know that the story of the Samaritan woman at the well was a shadow of the Gentile church, and in that story in John 4:40, *"He stayed **two days**. And because of His words many more became believers."* Yes, Jesus has stayed with His church this past two thousand years in the person of the Holy Spirit.

This same two thousand year period is obviously described differently for the Jews. An example of this in a "day shadow" is found in Hosea 6:2, which reads, *"After two days He will revive us; on the third day He will restore us, that we may live in His presence."* Please realize, though, that for Jews who believe in Jesus as their Savior now, they are a part of the true church of Christ. The above "two day" shadow was prophesied for the nation of Israel as a whole. Also remember that Romans 11:26 teaches us that *"All Israel will be saved."*

A shadow about the entire six day period from Adam until Jesus comes the second time, in His glory following the tribulation, is found in Matthew 17:1, *"After six days Jesus took with Him Peter, James and John, the brother of James, and led them up on a high mountain by themselves."* This scripture is the beginning of the story in which Jesus is miraculously changed right before His disciples' eyes and, *"There He was transformed before them. His face shone like the sun, and His clothes became white as the light."* Matthew 17:2.

Interestingly, another shadow has to do with the entire seven thousand year period of mankind in God's time line prior to heaven. We need to know first that in God's Word yeast always represents sin. The verse that covers the entire seven thousand year period from Adam to the end of Christ's Millennial Reign is found in Leviticus 23:6 in which God is outlining the Feast of Unleavened Bread, *"For seven days you are to eat bread made without yeast."* Obviously God's desire is that mankind does not sin during the entire seven thousand years. After that, after the Millennial Kingdom, sin itself will be impossible anyway.

Finally, are there any "day shadows" concerning the eighth day, heaven? The answer is a resounding, yes. My favorite is again found in the description of one of the feasts, which are always prophetic, for God's Word tell us in Colossians 2:16-17, *"with regard to a religious festival ... These are a shadow of the things that were to come."*

The eighth day shadow I like the most is found in the Feast of Tabernacles, described in Leviticus 23:35-44. In it the Hebrews were instructed to leave their homes and live in booths, or tents, for seven days. The Bible consistently uses tents to describe our bodies, such as in 2 Corinthians 5:1, *"Now we know that if the earthly tent we live in is destroyed ... "* And in describing the Feast of Tabernacles, God commands in Leviticus 23:42, *"Live in booths* (tents) *for **seven days.** "*

Leviticus 23:36 instructs, *"On the **eighth day** hold a sacred assembly and present an offering made to the Lord by fire."* This itself is a shadow of the future because we know that after the Millennial Reign of Christ *"The elements will be destroyed by fire."* This will be done in order to cleanse the world of all evil that it had been subjected to during the first seven thousand years, the first seven days. Yes, even during the Millennial Reign of Christ, sin will still be present, even though Satan will be held at bay during that time. But getting back to the Feast of Tabernacles, after the seven days are up, on the eighth day, the people were to leave their tents and return to their real home. And we, too, after the seven days of God's time line are up, will be going to our real home in heaven.

Dear Reader, the end of the first "six days" are upon us. The hard parts of the time line are behind. What is left is the glorious thousand year reign of Jesus, and then heaven itself. We will be a part of the best two days of God's time line. All we have to do is make Jesus the Lord of our lives. If for some reason you have not done that yet, do it this instant. Don't delay a minute. God's day calender is about to change from day six to day seven. When the day six page turns, the opportunity ends to be able to be a part of days seven and eight. Don't miss the two most wonderful days of the time line. Make Jesus Lord now. I'll see you on day seven.

Forgotten

There is a point of controversy you may be aware of that starts in 1 Kings 6, where we are told that Solomon began to build the temple in the 480th year after the children of Israel came out of the land of Egypt. The controversy stems from the fact that in Acts 13 Paul gives the chronology of this same period as 40 years in the wilderness, 450 years under the judges, and 40 years under the reign of Saul, making a total of 530 years. On top of that we have to add the 40 years of David's reign and the first three years of Solomon's rule before he actually started the temple. That makes 573 years for the exact same 480 year period described in Kings.

Biblical critics, of course, point to this as being an error in the Bible. Understandably they are happy to point out that our Bible is really messed up if the book of Kings says 480 years and the book of Acts says 573 years to describe the exact same period of history.

What very few people pay attention to is the fact that during this time period God gives up the Israelites again and again in punishment for their persistent idolatry. In fact, during this 573 time period they became slaves to Mesopotamia for 8 years, Moab for 18, the Canaanites for 20, the Midianites for 7, and finally the Philistines for 40 years. Those periods of slavery add up to 93 years, which if subtracted from the total 573 years brings us back to the 480 figure mentioned in Kings. Every year the Jews had been cast off by God had been completely eliminated in the book of Kings.

Now, let's look at the 70 week prophesy in Daniel. Obviously to anyone familiar with that prophesy, the first 69 weeks were fulfilled exactly to the day on the day Jesus entered Jerusalem on a donkey. It is also obvious, because Jesus made reference to it when asked in Matthew 24, that the 70th week would be the sign of His second coming. Jesus specifically mentions the abomination of desolation, which would occur in the middle of the 70th week according to the prophesy in Daniel, as being the definitive sign.

The idea that the delay between the 69th and 70th week was the time period needed to bring in the Gentiles is commonly taught. And we know from Paul that the eyes of the Israelites were purposefully blinded during this time in order that this church age could occur.

What we need to grab hold of is the truth that "God not only forgives, but he also forgets" is an actual fact. The 93 years and the time of the delay between the 69th and 70th weeks, the time periods God has ostracized His chosen people, have literally been forgotten. Allow that to sink in. God does not remember them, just like He promised. He not only forgot the 93 years in which He put the Israelites into bondage as punishment, but He also forgot the 2,000 years that He has kept them blinded to the truth so that we Gentiles could be saved.

This revelation has given birth to another one for me, one which is more personal, and therefore more meaningful. Just as the forgetting of those times by God for the Jews is literal, so the forgetting of my sins, as told to me in my favorite Old Testament chapter, Psalm 103, is just as literally true. There is not an inkling of a possibility that God will remember my sins. I mean, they are gone. My sins in God's eyes are gone.

Of course, I knew that my sins were covered by the blood of our Lord, and therefore unseen by the Father, and I had read over and over that they were forgotten, but now I *know* what that means. I have an even clearer, and more deeply rooted knowledge in the meaning of my sins being "forgotten." To God, all my past sins absolutely do not exist, and never will. The same is true of your sins. Phenomenal.

The next time anyone, including you or I, brings up their past sins, and the guilt that they still carry with them, we have a more clear biblical example of what "forgotten" really means. And since God has forgotten, they should as well, and move on.

Likewise, since we are to strive daily to be more Christlike, the next time we consider even thinking about the wrong that someone has done to us in the past, we need to stop and remember what "forgive and forget" means to our Lord, and in the same manner we need to forget just as completely.

What a phenomenal thing it is to be a child of God. How constantly thankful we all should be. His love for us is truly beyond description.

Secret Name Message

I imagine that you, like me, are intrigued by the many different messages God has hidden in His Word through the use of all sorts of different kinds of codes. One of the easiest to look for is the Hebrew meanings for names that are in the scriptures. A simple one is the story conveyed by the meaning of the name Barabbas, which is "son of the father," with Bar being "son of" and abba being an intimate name for father, kind of like Daddy. In that one name we saw that Jesus was crucified so that the "sons of the Father," namely you and I, could be set free.

Sometimes entire sentences are formed by looking at the names in a list. For instance, in my first book we found that the ten names in the first genealogy in the Bible phenomenally translate into the message, "Man is appointed mortal sorrow, but blessed God shall come down, teaching that His death shall bring the despairing comfort." How mind boggling is it to realize that in the very first genealogy in Genesis God had laid out the plan of our salvation?

Let's therefore look at what message God hid for us to uncover in the entire genealogy of Jesus. The first genealogy of Jesus is found in Matthew, but it begins with Abraham. So lets add to that the missing names from Adam up to Abraham that are found in the genealogy listed in Luke. At the end of this section I will give you the definitions of each of those individual names, but rather than keeping you in suspense, let's read the astounding and glorious hidden message:

"Man is appointed mortal sorrow, but blessed God shall come down, teaching that His death shall bring the despairing comfort. The fame of the stronghold of Babylon (representing evil) and its boundaries extend like a plant beyond the region of division at the tower of Babel. A Friend branches out, snorting with fury. The Exalted Father, the Father of a great multitude, laughs triumphantly, as He outwits His enemy. Praise breaks forth into an area surrounded by a wall of great height where the people of the Prince (representing Jesus) are safe from the false prophet (representing Satan), being clothed with strength. A Servant (Jesus) there is, One well loved, peaceful, who enlarges the people! My Father is Lord, the healer of the One whom the Lord judged and whom the Lord raised up! My strength and help are in the Lord. The Lord is perfect! I took hold of the strength of the Lord, and God made me forget my misery. The Master Builder, whom the Lord healed, and whom the Lord appointed, did uphold, and will uphold! I have asked God about the seed in Babylon. My father is majestic! God will raise up a Helper! The Just One will the Lord raise up! God is my praise! God is the Helper! May the gift of Israel increase, for God is with us!"

Wow!!! The deeper we dig into the treasure we possess known as the Bible, the more we find that we uncover the same message over and over; Jesus is our Savior. That plan was put in place before the beginning of the world.

What an incredible book is our Bible. We find the

same message in the surface text and in all of the other hidden messages, whether they are shadows, types, name or number codes, ELS codes, or any of the other myriad of coding devices we now know are within the body of the scriptures. With no pun intended, I submit that we are only now beginning to scratch the surface of how intricately woven throughout the Bible is the main theme; Jesus is our Savior and Lord. How unbelievably fortunate we are.

As promised, I will now list the names in the complete genealogy of Jesus, along with their meanings that form the spine tingling message we read above. Some names, of course, have two or three meanings, such as Adam meaning both "man" and "first blood." Naturally we took the meaning that seemed the most obviously to have been intended by God in His hidden message to us.

Adam means man, Seth - is appointed, Enosh - mortal, Kenan - sorrow, Mahalalel - blessed God, Jared - shall come down, Enoch - teaching that, Methuselah - His death shall bring, Lamech - the despairing, Noah - comfort. Shem - the fame of, Arphaxad - the stronghold of Babylon and its boundaries, Shelah - extend like a plant, Eber - beyond the region, Peleg - of division at the tower of Babel, Reu - a friend, Serug - branches out, Nahor -snorting, Terah - with fury, Abram/Abraham - the exalted father, the father of a great multitude, Isaac - laughs triumphantly, Jacob/Israel - he outwits his enemy, Judah - praise, Perez - breaks forth, Hezron - into an area surrounded by a wall, Ram - of great height, Amminadab - where the people of the prince are safe, Nahshon - from the false prophet, Salmon - being clothed, Boaz -strength, Obed - a servant, Jesse - there is, David - one well loved, Solomon -peaceful, Rehoboam - who enlarges the people, Abijah - my father is Lord, Asa - the healer, Jehoshaphat - of the one whom the Lord judged, Jehoram -and whom the Lord raised up, Uzziah - my strength and help are in the Lord, Jotham - the Lord is perfect, Ahaz - I took hold of, Hezekiah - the strength of the Lord, Manasseh - God made me forget my misery, Amon - the master builder, Josiah - whom the Lord healed, Jeconiah - whom the Lord appointed, did uphold, and will uphold, Shealtiel - I have asked God about, Zerubbabel -the seed in Babylon, Abiud - my father is majestic, Eliakim - God will raise up, Azor - a helper, Zadok - the just one, Akim - will the Lord raise up, Eliud - God is my praise, Eleazar - God is the helper, Matthan - may the gift of, Jacob - Israel, Joseph - increase, Jesus - God is with us.

There has never been any book that comes near the awesomeness of the Bible. I am convinced that we will be studying the intricate messaging within its pages until the end of the Millennial Kingdom.

Hilasterion

Our modern Bibles are so close to the original text that it is almost miraculous. God has seen to it through the ages that what He wanted conveyed is in fact what is being conveyed to us in His Word. Very rarely, though, there was an original word that might have lost a little bit in the translation to our less detailed English language. One of those words was the Greek word, hilasterion, which we find in its full form twice in the Bible.

The first time it is translated as "propitiation" or "sacrifice of atonement" in our modern versions. This is used to describe Jesus Himself in Romans 3:25, *"God presented Him* (Jesus) *as a **sacrifice of atonement**."* In this verse we see Jesus as the sacrificial substitute for our sins. The other time hilasterion is used it is translated as what is commonly known as the mercy seat, which was the top covering of the Ark of the Covenant. This is seen in Hebrews 9:5, *"Above the ark were the cherubim of glory, overshadowing the **atonement cover**."* This can be seen as the covering by mercy, again describing Jesus.

The reason I bring this word up, however, has to do with another word in our modern Bibles. First we need to know that our modern word "hilarious" comes from the root word, hilaron, from which hilasterion is derived. The point I am getting to is that the word "cheerful" found in 2 Corinthians 9:7 was originally hilaron. The verse reads in our Bibles. *"God loves a **cheerful** giver."*

God was definitely talking about our monetary giving in that chapter, but I wonder, was God really telling us to be a cheerful or hilarious giver, or was He telling us He wanted us to be a more Christ like and more sacrificial giver? It may seem like a very minor point, but is it? I think it may be worth pondering.

Shadows in Denial

I was looking at Peter's denial of Jesus three times the night Jesus was arrested in relationship to the verbal interchange between Peter and Jesus after His resurrection. Let's read that final conversation below:

"When Jesus and the disciples had finished eating, Jesus spoke to Simon Peter. He asked, 'Simon, son of John, do you really love me more than these others do?"

'Yes, Lord,' he answered. 'You know that I love you.'

Jesus said, 'Feed my lambs.'

Again Jesus asked, 'Simon, son of John, do you really love me?'

He answered, 'Yes, Lord. You know that I love you.'

Jesus said, 'Take care of my sheep.'

Jesus spoke to him a third time. He asked, 'Simon, son of John, do you love me?'

Peter felt bad because Jesus asked him the third time, "Do you love me?" He answered, 'Lord, you know all things. You know that I love you.'

Jesus said, 'Feed my sheep. What I'm about to tell you is true. When you were younger, you dressed yourself. You went wherever you wanted to go. But when you are old, you will stretch out your hands. Someone else will dress you. Someone else will lead you where you do not want to go." John 21:15-19.

Notice that Peter had denied Jesus three times the

night of the arrest, and in these scriptures Jesus makes Peter tell Him that he loves him three times. Obviously there is a shadow here. In fact, there may be several, but what I see is a picture of the three big denials of God by Israel. First, when Israel leaves the promised land and goes into Egypt (The World), God shows His love and brings them out in the whole story of Moses. Second, Israel turns to idols and God has to send them into captivity in Babylon, from which he eventually brings them out. Third, Israel denies Jesus as their Messiah when He comes the first time. Their eyes are then blinded (as Jesus tells Peter his eyes will be), but of course He will again save them at His second coming.

An interesting side note and the point that strikes me is that the three times Jesus asked Peter if he loved Him, there were actually two different Greek words used for love. The first one was more like a friendship love, or being fond of. It was "phileo." The second word for love was more like a Godly love or divine love. It is "agape." The first two times Jesus asked Peter if he loved Him He used the word "agape" and Peter answered with "phileo." The last time Jesus used the word "phileo," not "agape," and Peter also answered with "phileo."

Could it be that since Jesus used phileo the last time, it was a shadow of His coming back at the end of the tribulation as King instead of Savior, with the true salvation of the Jewish nation being at the end of the Millennial Kingdom, the seventh day? Remember, this was foreshadowed in the Feast of Tabernacles in which the Jews are instructed to live in tents or booths for seven days and then they get to go to their real home on the eighth day (The end of the Millennial Kingdom when they will enter heaven). This again seems to make sense to me in line with the prophecy that the animal sacrifices will continue to be so important during the Millennial Kingdom, as we are told that they will be in the last chapters of Ezekiel.

It may not be an extremely important point for us, the church, but it is an interesting point to ponder.

Strange?

I have been reading the sermons of Peter Marshall, the wonderful minister and Chaplain of the US Senate who was portrayed after his death in the very popular book and movie of the early 1950's, "A Man Called Peter."

In one of his sermons he relates a story from <u>Rough Justice</u>, by C.E. Montague. The story is so profound that I thought it should be shared. It deserves our full attention so I will quote it here word for word:

"One of the memorable scenes in an English novel of some years ago describes how a little boy named Bron goes to church for the first time with his governess.

He watches with interest every part of the service and then the preacher climbs into the high pulpit and Bron hears him give out a piece of terrible news.

It is about a kind and brave man who was nailed to a cross…. ferociously hurt a long time ago…. who feels a dreadful pain even now, because there was something not done that he wants them all to do.

Little Bron thinks that the preacher is telling the story because a lot of people are there and they will do something about it.

Bron is sitting impatiently on the edge of the pew. He can hardly wait to see what the first move will be in righting this injustice. But he sits quietly and decides that after the service someone will do something about it.

Little Bron weeps…. but nobody else seems at all

upset. The service is over, the people walk away as if they had not heard the terrible news, as if nothing remarkable had happened.

As Bron leaves the church, he is trembling.

His governess looks at him and says 'Bron, don't take it to heart - someone will think you are strange."

Oh, for us all to feel like Bron. Oh, for us all to be "strange". I know I'm not "strange" enough. There are people who I know who are not saved that I have not talked with yet about Jesus. You and I were not given the future of a wonderful eternity with God just so we could sit around feeling secure and being thankful, while others around us are lost. Yes, the politically correct thing to do is to not intrude on others' beliefs. But a soul's eternal future is way too important to stand on political correctness. It is so important that it is worth being "strange". What about you? Are you strange?

Asheville Airport

I grew up in the small mountain town of Brevard, N.C. It is located at the western point of a triangle formed by Hendersonville, 22 miles to the southeast, and Asheville, 32 miles to the northeast. The airport for the area is the Asheville Airport which is about half way between Hendersonville and Asheville.

About nine or ten years ago Barb and I moved from Florida to Greenville, S.C., which is about an hour to the south of Hendersonville. As you can imagine, we often drive up to the mountains on little Saturday afternoon getaways. When we do, as we pass the airport on interstate 26 between Hendersonville and Asheville, I commonly find myself musing about an airplane accident that very nearly occurred almost forty years ago on I-26 at an overpass less than a mile from the airport. It is a story that I hope I never forget.

In July, 1971, Florence Moore, of Yoakum, Texas, heard the bad news that her mother was dying of cancer. Since her mom lived in Hendersonville, N.C., there were continual long drives from Texas to N.C. to be with her mom during the final months. On one of the trips, Florence's husband, David, decided that Florence should stay with her mom and he would take the bus back to Texas for a week or so. Fortunately for David, who hated that bus trip, his friend, Henry Gardner, offered to fly David back to Hendersonville in his little Cessna 180.

The flight was terrible from the outset. As soon as they got to Houston they encountered pea soup fog that seemed to last forever and ever. To make matters worse, when they reached Jackson, Mississippi, the plane's radio and instruments failed completely. Lady Luck arrived just as panic was setting in with both David and Henry because the fog lifted, and when they looked through the clearing they could see an airport directly in front of them. Landing the Cessna, they found a mechanic and got a bite of lunch. Soon the pair were back in the air with their instruments and radio working fine and a fresh tank of fuel.

All was well as they passed Atlanta, but when they flew by Greenville, S.C., the sky started turning gray again. Pushing on, however, they made it past the first ridge of mountains that Barb and I get to view to the north as we drive around Greenville. Beyond that mountain range, though, on their last leg into the Asheville Airport, an anxious David and Henry ran into another wall of fog. It was at this point that Henry radioed the Asheville Airport control tower for instructions.

The drama that was to transpire was fortunately recorded later by Joan Anderson. Rather than trying to describe the next hair raising minutes myself, lets read Ms. Anderson's report. We'll start with the exact words Henry and David heard from the air-traffic controller in the Asheville tower that fateful day,

"Our field is closed because of the fog and we have no capability for instrument landing. Return to Greenville and land there.'

'But I can't,' Henry protested. 'We're almost out of fuel - we won't have enough to fly back to Greenville.'

There was silence. Then, 'okay,' the radio voice snapped. 'We'll get the ground crew ready. Come in on an emergency landing.'

David gripped the sides of his seat. They seemed to be flying in a dense gray blanket, and the Asheville control tower couldn't possibly see them. How were he and Henry going to land? Henry reassured David, and after a brief scan of the blueprint, he began his blind descent. The airport runway *should* be beneath them - but what if it wasn't?

Suddenly a voice came over the radio: 'Pull it up! Pull it up!'

Henry immediately pulled up on the stick. As he did so, the men saw a split in the fog, and the view beneath sent tremors of fear through each of them. Instead of being over the runway, they were above an interstate highway! Had they descended a few feet farther, they would have hit a bridge and certainly crashed.

The two looked at each other. They were almost out of fuel, and inside the grayness it was impossible to know where they were. Henry tried to descend again, but almost hit the tips of some trees poking above the fog. Again he pulled up sharply. There seemed to be no way out of their dilemma. Without enough fuel - or guidance from the control tower - how could they possibly land?

Then, with enormous relief, they heard the controller's composed voice breaking into the tense silence in the cockpit. 'If you will listen to me,' he said, 'I'll help you get down.'

'Go ahead,' Henry radioed back in relief.

The controller began his instructions. 'Come down just a little,' he said. 'Now over to the right. Down a little more....'

David gripped the seat, praying intently. Thank God the controller had been able to pick them up on radar, despite the airport's apparent lack of the necessary instruments. But would they make it on time? It seemed impossible. The fuel needle was hovering on E, but the voice went on with calm authority; 'Not so fast. Easy, easy now....' Was the nightmare flight ever going to end? And would he see his wife and daughter again?

'Raise it up a little now. No, you're too far to the left.' The journey seemed to be taking forever. But all of a sudden the controller said, 'You're right over the end of the runway. Set it down ... now!'

Obediently, Henry dropped the plane through the fog, and the two men recognized the beginning of a runway just ahead, with lights along both sides. It was the most welcomed sight they had ever seen. Within minutes they touched down. Tears of gratitude and relief filled David's eyes when he saw Florence standing at the end of the runway.

The plane taxied to a stop, and the two men offered a prayer of thanksgiving. Then Henry turned the radio on again. 'Thanks so much,' he told the air traffic controller, his voice shaky with relief. 'You probably saved our lives.'

But the controllers response stopped both men in their tracks. 'What are you talking about? We lost all radio contact with you when we told you to return to Greenville.'

'You what?' Henry asked, incredulous.

"We never heard from you again, and we never heard you talking to us or to anyone else.' The controller told them. 'We were stunned when we saw you break through the clouds."*

*From: <u>Where Angels Walk</u>, by Joan Anderson.

On the Throne

Revelation 3:21 is a verse that causes me to say "WOW" out loud. As you know, the letters that Jesus wrote to the seven churches in Revelation were not only written to seven actual churches, but are commonly thought to have been written to Christians in the seven ages of the Church, with Ephesus representing the Apostolic Church, which was the church up to 100 AD, Smyrna representing the Age of Persecution, which was 100 AD to 313 AD, Pergamos being the Imperial Church age from 313 AD to 590 AD, Thyatira being the Age of Papacy from 590 AD to 1517 AD, Sardis being the Age of Reformation from 1517 AD to 1730 AD, Philadelphia the Age of Missions from 1730 AD to 1900 AD, and finally Laodicea being the modern church age, from 1900 AD to the year Christ returns.

All of the seven letters end with a promise from Jesus as to what the Christians of that time would receive if they "overcame". All of the promises are exciting, from being given the right to eat from the tree of life, to being given a "white stone", which represents celebrity status such as Greek Olympic athletes had. They are all wonderful rewards to be given in heaven.

When it comes to Laodicea, the letter written to us, the emphasis always seems to be on the fact that Jesus said the church of our time was neither hot nor cold, and that since our church as a whole was lukewarm, Jesus said he was going to spit it out of His mouth. But let's really look at the promise for those of us who overcome.

I am bowled over by it. Here it is, from Revelation 3:21: *"To him who overcomes, I will give the right to sit with me on my throne, just as I overcame and sat down with my Father on His throne."*

Let that sink in. It is one of the most incredible things you may ever read. If we only overcome Satan and the world for the few relatively short years we live on this earth, we will actually sit down with Jesus on His throne, for eternity. Can you imagine what that would be like. Talk about being born into royalty. WOW !!!

Of course, if someone doesn't believe in a literal heaven, that may not mean much. But if we are truly a Christian, we must believe that heaven is a real place, just like Borneo is a real place even though we haven't seen it with our own eyes. If we don't believe it, we are saying that Jesus is a liar. For me, Jesus said over and over that heaven exists, so end of debate.

Therefore, if heaven exists, the throne Jesus sits on exists, and you and I can earn the right to actually sit on it with Jesus. The thought sends chills up my spine. All we have to do is "overcome". Whatever that takes, no matter what, the reward is a billion times greater than the acts involved in overcoming. If ever we could be persuaded not to give 100% of our love and our lives to Jesus, that should dissolve with the realization of what that verse is saying. There could be no greater promise than that. That is the best there is.

Whatever this world or Satan throws at you, remember the vision of you sitting right beside Jesus on his throne. For such a reward, there is nothing you or I could not withstand. Burn it in your memory. Don't ever forget it.

I will look forward to shaking your hand, with a big grin on my face from ear to ear, when you and I sit down together, of all places, on the throne of Jesus, right along side Him. Talk about a front row seat to the events of eternity. Words don't come close.

The Beyond Awesome Bible

After reading this you may never look at your Bible the same way again.

Although there is still some controversy surrounding ELS codes in the Bible, what I am going to share with you should end the controversy. For anyone still not aware of ELS codes, they refer to the strange fact that words, phrases, complete sentences, and even paragraphs are now being found by high speed computers underneath the surface Hebrew and Greek text of God's Word in "equidistant letter sequence, or spacing." For example, a complete paragraph may be written underneath the normal body of the scriptures, spelled out with every seventh letter. Obviously, the longer and more complicated the ELS code, the less the chance is that it could happen by random chance.

Today I want to look at two ways God linked the books of the Bible with ELS coding. First, lets examine an unusual phenomenon in the Torah, the first five books of the Bible. Between Genesis and Exodus the Hebrew word for torah is found in an ELS with the first letters at the end of Genesis and the remaining letters at the beginning of Exodus. Next, Exodus and Leviticus are linked in the same manner with an ELS of the word torah. In the very middle of Leviticus is an ELS spelling out torah. Then interestingly we find that the two books of Leviticus and Numbers are also linked with torah, but this time torah is spelled backwards. The same is true of Numbers and Deuteronomy, the last two of the five books in the Torah. So torah is spelled forward linking the first two books and Leviticus, and backwards linking the last two books and Leviticus, with torah spelled normally in the center of Leviticus. The first two books and the last two books all have torah pointing toward the center of the Torah. The chances of that happening by random chance is said by experts to be "incalculable."

Next, let's look at the Bible as a whole. Skeptics always say that the Bible is just a collection of books put together by man. How wrong they are. I hope you are sitting down for this because it will blow you away. The truth is that all sixty six books of the Bible are linked together with the name "Yeshua" (Jesus). Let that sink in. The word Yeshua starts at the end of Genesis and ends in an ELS code in Exodus. It does the exact same thing sixty five times, linking every one of the sixty six books in the exact order they are found in our Bible.

To put that in prospective, recently a trillion dollars has been bandied around in the news quite a bit, and it was figured that a trillion one dollar bills stacked on top of each other would stretch sixty thousand miles. But if we want to take a similar picture of the random chance of the name Yeshua linking all sixty six books of the Bible, we would need to pile sheets of thin tissue paper to the very end of the universe, putting a red dot on only one of those sheets and then picking it out blindfolded by random chance. A person would have to randomly choose the one and only correct sheet to prove that it was remotely possible for anything other than God having linked all of those sixty six books in order by equidistant letters sequencing with the name of Jesus.

We must treasure and revere our Bible with the awe it deserves. It was written totally, letter by letter, by the all divine God who created everything, including the uninformed skeptic himself. God's Word may be the most complex creation of all time, and from Genesis to Revelation Jesus is the focal point.

Born as a Lamb

We are all familiar with the scripture in Luke 2 that says about the birth of Jesus that *"the shepherds were keeping watch over their flock by night."* What makes no sense is the part, *"by night."* The reason I say that is that we know that the flocks did not graze at night. In reality they were brought into caves that existed on the hillside overlooking Bethlehem. A hedge was then put at the cave entrance to keep the sheep in and the wolves out. There was only one exception, that being a few flocks of lambs that did graze at night beside the road that passed by Bethlehem going to Jerusalem. Those lambs were sold to people passing on that road early in the morning to be used as sacrifices later in the day in Jerusalem. The fact is that the angels recorded in Luke came to announce the birth of Jesus to shepherds whose duty it was to watch over the lambs that were to be the passover sacrifices.

Of course Jesus was born in a stable because there was no room in the inn. Bethlehem was small and there may have only been one inn at that time. At any rate, the stable referred to did not look like a stable we see in pictures. In reality it would have been one of those hillside caves I just mentioned. So Jesus was born in the same place those sacrificial lambs were born.

Incidentally, the Hebrew word that we read as "swaddling clothes" was actually the word that described some very cheap cloth that was used to wrap the lambs in as soon as they were born.

The description of Jesus being the Lamb of God sent as a sacrifice to take away the sins of the world can be seen very dramatically in His very birth. His story began in a cave on a Bethlehem hillside where other lambs were born for only one reason, to serve as a passover sacrifice. Jesus was the Lamb of God whose passover sacrifice once and for all gave us eternal life.

Poison Pen Letter

We are so fortunate. Since you are reading this book, I am assuming that you, like me, are not really persecuted for being a Christian. We may be running into more opposition today than we did in the past, but persecution is not the description of it. Sadly, that is not the case everywhere.

In fact, I am holding in my hand at this moment a letter that is being sent right now to thousands of our Christian brothers and sisters in a particular nation. Consider your emotions if you received this actual letter in the mail, as others like us are this week in September, 2010:

IN THE NAME OF ALLAH,
AND OF HIS FINAL PROPHET, MOHAMMAD
(PEACE BE UPON HIM):
The true religion of Islam **WILL ARISE** in your area; you can not stop Allah's will.

We have been watching your family; we have seen you go to church and seen you pray to your false god. We know that you are infidels, and we will deal with you as our holy Quran declares:

In Sura 9 verse 5, it says **TO SLAY** the idolaters wherever you find them; take them captive and besiege them.

It also says in Sura 9 verse 29 to **FIGHT** those who

have been given the scripture and believe not in Allah or the Last Day or follow not the religion of truth.

If you and your entire family do not leave your false religion and follow Islam, you will be killed. Your sons will be slaughtered and your daughters will become Muslim wives, bearing sons who will fight for Allah in this region.

Your ONLY other option is to **FLEE TONIGHT,** Leave your home and everything behind.

ALLAHU AKBAR!

At the bottom of the letter I am in possession of is a picture of a bullet. Can you imagine what must be going through the minds of our fellow Christians as they read these letters and think of their children. It must be chilling.

Your first thought as you read the above letter was probably the same as mine, pure anger against those who are sending it. However, I am not reporting this to make you mad at the Muslims who are the perpetrators of such hatred and fear. I am including this information and actual letter, including its misspelling, to encourage us to immediately pray three things.

First, we should pray that our Christian brothers and sisters be given wisdom to know what they should do. Second, we should pray that God protects them and their families. And third, we should pray for those who are sending the letters, those who are being held in darkness by Satan in such a demonic religion. It is never to late. Muslims are coming to Jesus in record numbers. Those who are sending such fear and hate can still be saved. Satan has deceived them. Our prayers could make the difference.

Bronze

History is pretty fuzzy about the period of time that the Bible chronicles from Adam to the flood. Have you ever wondered if there is any way to see if what little historical data there is for those years might coincide with Biblical accounts? Let's look at one obscure scripture from that period and "search out the matter."

The fourth chapter of Genesis tells us about the descendants of Cain, of Cain and Abel fame. Verse 22 says, *"Zillah also had a son, Tubal-Cain, who forged all kinds of tools out of bronze and iron."* That may be interesting reading but is there a reason God would have included it in His Word? As with virtually every sentence in the Bible, we might be surprised at what we might find if we dig deeper.

The Holy Scriptures are chocked full of things like numbers of years a person lived, and ages of people when they had their first son, etc. From these Biblical statements the Israelites came up with their calendar, using the creation of Adam as its beginning. According to the Hebrew calendar we are now in year 5770.

Getting back to "searching out the matter" in the selected verse that tells us that Tubal-Cain forged tools out of bronze, the Bible does not give us years and ages for his lineage from Cain up to him, but it does list his ancestors by name. His mother was Zillah and his father was Lamech, his grandfather was Methushael, and before them came Mehujael, Irad, Enoch, Cain and Adam. The subject of our search, Tubal-Cain, was the last in the line prior to the flood, which wiped out all of Cain's descendants.

If we look at Seth, Cain's brother, we can trace his descendants up to Noah, and since the age of the father at each son's birth is given, we can even come up with a date for the flood, when our hero, Tubal-Cain, obviously died. To be exact, Adam and Eve had Seth when Adam was 130, Seth had Enosh at age 105, Enosh had Kenan at age 90, Kenan had Mahalalel at age 70, who had Jared at 65, who had Enoch at 162, who had Methusaleh at 65, who had Lamech at 187, who had Noah at 182. Noah was 600 when the flood came.

Using a mid point of Noah's 600 years before the flood we can add up those numbers and come up with about 1,350 years after the arrival of Adam for Tubal-Cain to be working in his home made bronze tool factory. By subtracting 1,350 years from today's Jewish year of 5770 we find ourselves back at about 2400 BC when the Bible asserts that Tubal-Cain was forging all kinds of tools with bronze. What is so fascinating about that is that of all of the millions and millions of bronze age artifacts that have been uncovered by archeologists and carbon dated, the oldest dates back to the same date of 2400 BC.

The Bible is always 100% accurate. Always. Since we know that science does occasionally make mistakes, rather than science being used to prove the Bible, scientists should look to the Bible to prove their findings. The Bible is always 100% accurate. Always.

A Crowded Church

We are told in 1 Peter 1:12 that *"Even angels long to look into these things"* that have been told to us by those who preach the gospel.

And then we find in Ephesians 3:10 an extremely interesting but unheralded scripture that says, *"..to the extent that now the manifold wisdom of God might be made known by the church to the principalities and powers in the heavenly places."*

The *"principalities and powers"* referred to in that verse are angels. Notice how they now learn about *"the manifold wisdom of God."* It is *"by the church."*

W.A. Criswell said, "Just the idea of it is astonishing: that the angels in heaven are taught the manifold wisdom of God by the church. What an amazing discovery!"

So next Sunday, when you are in church, you can ponder the Biblical fact that there are angels sitting there with you, probably listening even more intently than you are. It truly is an amazing discovery.

Six Days

There was a portion of the original manuscript of Unlocking God's Secrets that did not make it into the published book because the publisher was concerned that it would be so controversial in some Christian circles that they would not allow their flocks to read the rest of the book. He may have been correct in his assessment; however, there is another point that may have been even more important that I want to correct today.

By omitting the truth of that unpublished portion we may have inadvertently continued to push the unbeliever in God away from the total truth of His existence, because our silence in the matter once again made the atheist feel that since we Christians as a whole teach one thing that flies in the face of known and proven reality, anything else we say about the Bible must be taken with the utmost skepticism. Rather than beating around the bush, let me get right into the heart of the matter.

Up until 1950 most of the non believing scientists subscribed to what is known as the "steady state theory," which basically taught that the universe as we know it had existed eternally. Everything changed with the idea of the "big bang theory." This theory is widely held today as truth and is based on the thought that everything started at a particular point in time.

God told us in His very first sentence, *"In the beginning God created the heavens and the earth."* Genesis 1:1. But what about believing and being adamant that God created everything in six 24 hour days? I will state here, much to the raised eyebrows of some of my believing friends, that God's Word is always accurate, but our insistence on the days being made up of normal earthly 24 hours is less than rational and often extremely harmful, because it drives away people who otherwise might be brought into the light of Christ. Please bear with me as I explain.

First of all, common sense will tell us that the days could not have been our solar days, since the sun and earth were not even listed in the creation story until "days" two and three, and yet God talks about what happened on day one. According to God's Word there simply was no earth making a 24 hour revolution, which is what our day is defined as. The earth did not exist. Period. Neither did the sun.

We need to also understand that the days could not represent our earthly thousand years, which some believers have tried to make fit, because once again, at the very beginning there were no earthly measures to even multiply by a thousand. Six thousand years do come into play, but in relation to end time prophecy, not in relation to time prior to our calendar dating, or the time that is referred to by scientists as cosmic proper time or CPR.

Science, however, is now aligning itself with everything that God said all along. Science took a giant leap forward in 1915 when Albert Einstein stunned the world with what is now known as fact, that there are changes in time flow dependant on gravity and velocity. This difference in the passing of time is known in scientific circles as "time dilation."

Most of us can understand how gravity affects our weight, but we haven't come to grips with how it can slow down time. Science, though, has proven that it does. The other thing that affects time is speed. The easiest way to understand it is to visualize waves of sound or light going out from a central gravitational point in space. They don't go in a straight line. They are "waves" because they go back and forth as they travel outward. The farther out they go, the farther back and forth they go in an increasingly widening arc. As they travel out, it takes longer to go a specific straight distance away from the original gravitational point because they are traveling ever and ever farther on their back and forth arcs. The end result is that in the second year they can only go half as far away from the starting point as they did in the first year. In the third year they go only half as far as they did in the second year. The reason again is that the farther out they go, the more back and forth on the wave arc they also have to go.

Our day is in reality a measure of distance. If the circumference of our earth were three times greater, and if the earth revolved at the same speed, it would obviously take three times longer to see the sun each revolution at any given spot on the earth as it does now. In that situation our day would be 72 hours long instead of 24 hours as it really is. The first CPR day, before there was an earth or sun, was also a matter of distance. It was a distance from the origin of the "big bang", or to state it simpler, the origin of the first explosion of energy. This is the point at the beginning when "God spoke" everything into being.

Scientists know that the "big bang" was an explosion of radiation, the basis of all forms of light. It has actually been named cosmic background radiation (CBR) and it was discovered by Arno Penzias and Robert Wilson in 1965. It is the only source of radiation that has existed since creation.

At the moment creation occurred, we know that the first "expulsion" of universe was a million million times hotter than black space is today, and it was a million million times smaller than it is today. It was a burst of energy beyond compare, and since, according to science, energy can neither be created nor destroyed, it had to come from somewhere. That "somewhere" was the voice of God. God spoke and everything was created.

But getting back to the six days, the energy traveled out, and according to Einstein's formula, $E=MC2$ (energy equals mass times the speed of light squared), mass or matter was created out of that energy. Actually it took a massive amount of energy to create a tiny amount of matter. So, matter was being created from "God spoke," which scientists look at as the initial burst of energy.

This sounds very complicated, but the main thing we need to understand is that the first cosmic day the energy, or light, traveled twice as far as it did the second cosmic day, so, since a CPR day was measured in distance, as ours is, the first cosmic day was twice as long as the second cosmic day, which in turn was twice as long as the third cosmic day, etc. Stated another way, since the energy traveled a shorter distance away from the source the second day, due to the widening back and forth arc, the second day was shorter by one half.

Genesis 1:3 says, *"And God said, 'Let there be light', and there was light. God saw that the light was good, and he separated the light from the darkness. God called the light 'day' and the darkness He called 'night.' And there was evening, and there was morning - the first day."*

An important aside is that the original Hebrew words in that scripture for *"evening"* and *"morning"* were Erev and boker. Erev actually refers to dark, obscure, randomness, or chaos. Boker is the advent of light which intimates that order begins to appear. So the last line of that quote more correctly should be translated as, "And there was chaos, and there was order - the first day."

Scientists tell us that after what they call the big bang (when God spoke), light did in fact separate from darkness, as electrons bonded to atomic nuclei, just as Genesis states. Galaxies started to form during this period, which took eight billion years. So eight billion years was the length of the first day of cosmic proper time (CPR).

The second day, therefore, would have lasted four billion years, since it would have had to have been about half the length of time of the first CPR day. During this second day, God's Word tells us He formed the firmament which He called "sky." The scientists tell us that during this four billion year period the Milky Way was formed, which obviously is our sky. God's Word was correct, as it always is.

During the third day, which lasted about two billion years (half the second day), the Bible says that the earth was formed with dry land and water, and vegetation began. Surprise, surprise, the scientists as one voice tells us that this is exactly what happened during this two billion year length of time.

During day four, in verses 14 through 19, God says, *"Let there be lights in the expanse of the sky to separate day from night."* He goes on to talk about the sun, moon and stars. The scientists tell us that during this one billion year period, the fourth CPR day, the earth's atmosphere became transparent, so the sun, moon, and stars were now visible from earth. The scientists and God are in total agreement again.

The Bible now tells us in verses 20 through 23 that God created fish and birds on the fifth day. Interestingly, that is exactly what scientists say happened during the next five hundred million years, the fifth CPR day.

The two hundred and fifty million years leading up to the beginning of Jewish dating, which would have been the sixth CPR day and the sixth day in the Bible, according to scientists were the years in which the large land mammals and humans first came on the scene. As we would expect, those are the exact things God said He created on the sixth day.

God's Word is exact. Every time. And science is unwittingly proving that fact. The reality is that the Bible is proving that some of the notions of modern science is correct. Scientists say that creation started at one point in space with a burst of energy that, according to their own laws, had to have come from an outside entity. They further state that the creation, or big bang, occurred about sixteen billion years ago, which they themselves break up into six cosmic proper time days. The big bang was God speaking, and those six CPR days are God's original six days. We just didn't know it until now.

Understanding the truth of the six days of creation does not lesson the miracle at all. In fact, for me, seeing the complexity of God's plan to create us, His ultimate object of love, makes the miracle of creation even more astonishing and awe inspiring. And by having a better understanding of this phenomenal miracle of creation we just might be able to eliminate a stumbling block of many unbelievers and bring those we love who are in the dark into the glorious light of the love of Jesus Christ, who *"by Him and for Him all things were created."* Colossians 1:16.

Bananas

Missionary Darlene Diebler tells in her autobiography, <u>Evidence Not Seen</u>, about her terrible time of abuse when she was held as a prisoner in a Japanese POW camp during World War II. She speaks of being near total starvation. At one point she saw through her cell window a banana in the far distance. "Lord," she prayed, "just one banana."

Darlene had read over and over in years past the blessed promise in Philippians 4:9, *"God shall supply all your need according to His riches in glory by Christ Jesus."* But that day they were just words. She had suffered enough in that camp, and been fed nothing but virtual water soup, that the promise and her prayer were not realities anymore. Prison life was.

The next day was the same horrible routine, as all the countless others before; until that is, she heard heavy footsteps down the hall, and the turning of a key in her cell door lock. A guard walked in with a bunch of bananas. "They're yours." he said, and stomped out.

Sitting in silence, with tears streaming down her face, Darlene counted bananas. All 92 of them.

In her heart that small voice whispered, "That's what I delight to do, exceedingly abundantly above everything you ask or think."

The Three Woman Bride

As you know by now, I am utterly in awe of the way God wove shadows of future events throughout the Bible. Seeing the abundance of them drives home the point to me that only our divine Creator could have written such a phenomenal book. Unfortunately, seldom do scholars ever seem to "search out" the shadows, other than a few obvious ones in the Old Testament that are included as pictures of the first coming of Christ. But shadows are just as plentiful in the New Testament as previews of what was to come following His resurrection.

We discussed in two earlier sections in this book the fact that the Samaritan woman and the Canaanite woman respectively were both shadows of the coming church. Both were Gentile women who interrupted Jesus as He was on His way to save the Jewish people. In the same manner the Gentile church has been a two thousand year interruption in God's quest to save His chosen children, the Hebrew nation.

In a well known story in Mark 5 we can see that another woman was just as surely a shadow of the church. The story I am referring to is the one in which a Jewish ruler, Jairus, asked Jesus to come to his house and save his dying daughter. On the way to the house Jesus was interrupted by the woman with the issue of blood. Because of that interruption the daughter of Jairus died before Jesus could reach the child.

Think about it. Jesus came to first save the Jewish people, as we learned in the story of the Canaanite woman, but that woman also interrupted His journey to complete His mission. In the same way the woman with the issue of blood interrupted Christ's journey to Jairus's house. Three women, all represented the coming church. Three women, all shadows of His bride. And all three women were shadows of this two thousand year church age interruption which has given us Gentiles the chance to enter paradise.

Fortunately for the Jewish people, in the end of the story in Mark 5, Jesus brings back to life the daughter of Jairus, obviously a shadow of what is still to come for the Hebrew nation, the nation that because of God's promises to the patriarchs is and forever will be His children.

What a remarkable treasure the Bible is. Cherish it. Study it. Put His Word in your heart daily. Nothing on earth compares to it.

Why Bethlehem

Have you ever wondered why God chose Bethlehem for the birthplace of His son? All three patriarchs, Abraham, Isaac and Jacob, were buried at Hebron. So were Sarah, Leah and Rebecca. Rachel, the wife of Jacob, however, was not buried there. She was buried on the Bethlehem Road below the caves in which Jesus was born. Rachel died giving birth to a son. As she was dying she named her son Ben-Oni, which means "Son of Sorrow." Jacob, the father, though, changed his name to Benjamin, which means "Son of my Right Hand." This is interesting because Jesus first came as "A man of sorrows," as described in Isaiah 53:3, but now we know that he is seated at the right hand of God. The Father in heaven changed Jesus from "Ben-Oni" to "Benjamin."

In Jeremiah 31 we are told that Rachel was mourning and weeping for her children because her children were no more. That was the case because they were in bondage. In verse 16, though, the Lord tells her to stop her weeping for they will return from the land of the enemy. That is something to ponder when we consider that she is the matriarch whose tomb is at the birthplace of Jesus.

A second possible reason for Bethlehem being the selected town was that the story of Ruth occurred there. You probably know that the story of Ruth is one of the classic "type and shadow" stories of the New Covenant of Jesus. Ruth was a gentile. Her mother in law, Naomi, was a Jew. And both went to Bethlehem and were saved by Naomi's relative, Boaz, who became the kinsman redeemer when he married Ruth. Of course, we will be redeemed by our "Kinsman Redeemer" at the marriage feast of the Lamb described in Revelation 19:9.

Going on, Ruth became the great, great grandmother of King David, whose father, Jesse, still lived in Bethlehem. From David, of course, was prophesied to be the lineage of the Messiah, which obviously came to pass.

Speaking of prophesy, no discussion of Bethlehem is complete without mentioning the famous prophesy from Micah 5:2 written some 500 years before Christ's birth that says, *"But you, Bethlehem, Efrathah, though you are small among the clans of Judah, out of you will come for me one who will be ruler over Israel, whose origins are from of old, from ancient times."*

Finally, the name Bethlehem comes from two Hebrew root words meaning "House of Bread". We only have to look at the words of Jesus himself who told us explicitly, *" I am the bread of life. He who comes to me will never go hungry, and he who believes in me will never be thirsty."* John 6:35.

Jesus added, *"For my Father's will is that everyone who looks to the Son and believes in Him shall have eternal life, and I will raise him up at that last day."* John 6:40.

Nothing God does is without reason or plan. Bethlehem was prepared in advance to be the birthplace of our Lord, just as the New Jerusalem has been prepared in advance in heaven to be our eternal home.

John 14

A lot of what I enjoy digging into and writing about deals with exciting things that are hidden within the Word of God. Things like "types and shadows" are fun to explore, and teach us about God, prophecy, and things God truly wants us to know. As He says, He wants us to *"search out the matter,"* and we are normally awe struck when we do.

In this section, however, I want to look at a chapter in God's true and definitive communication to us that may not have anything hidden in it. It surely could not be any more informative if it did, because this may be the one chapter in the Bible that clearly tells us everything we need to know about the absolute plan of God. This one chapter gives us as Christians our true "hope," and dare I say it, "our responsibility." And it was given to us by Jesus Himself. The chapter I am talking about is the fourteenth chapter of the Gospel of John. Let's look at a few of Jesus's own words from that incredible chapter.

"Trust in God - trust also in me." John 14:1.

Trust in Jesus. This is not a suggestion. This is a commandment.

"In my Father's house are many rooms. If it were not so I would have told you. I am going there to prepare a place for you. And if I go and prepare a place for you, I will come back and take you to be with me that you also may be where I am." John 14:2-3.

Heaven is not an ethereal place without physical properties. It is a real place, and Jesus Himself is preparing something special for us there, where we will actually have eternal life with Him. And He is promising to come back and take us there to live with Him. Our "hope" is not that Jesus will make things peachy keen for us here on earth, although he does help us in this earthly life. No, our "hope" is in an eternal life in a real place called heaven. That is what our focus should be on.

"I am the way and the truth and the life. No one comes to the Father except through me." John 14:6.

We can not get to heaven by being good. We can't get there by being Muslim or Buddhist or Hindu. There is no possible way of gaining eternal life in heaven except through Jesus. Our Savior could not have been more clear. The majority of the world is in for a huge shock. Jesus is the only option. Otherwise we perish.

"If you love me, you will obey what I command. And I will ask the Father, and he will give you another Counselor to be with you forever - the Spirit of truth." John 14:15-17.

We need to notice that the promise of the Holy Spirit that guides us and helps us in so many ways begins with a big word, "if." *"If you love me, you will obey what I command."* We must ask ourselves, how can we obey what Jesus commands unless we know what His commandments are? We can't. And the only way to know what He commands is to study what He says to us in the Bible. How many people who call themselves Christians have even read the words of Jesus in the New Testament? From what I see, the answer is relatively few. We are talking about the Holy Spirit here, God Himself. We are talking about eternal life. This is not a child's game. We are talking about the most important thing in each person's life, and it is sluffed off as something trivial. Jesus even reiterates this point.

"Whoever has my commands and obeys them, he is the one who loves me. He who loves me will be loved by my Father, and I too will love him and show myself to him." John 14:21.

Does Jesus need to hit us over the head with the same thought again. He must, because He goes on to say:

"If anyone loves me, he will obey my teaching. My Father will love him, and we will come to him and make our home with him." John 14:23.

Dear reader, heaven is real. This life is less than a split second compared to eternity. Jesus even said in John 6:63, *"The flesh counts for nothing."* Heaven is our goal. Heaven is our "hope." Jesus is the only way to get there. We are taught to love Him and obey Him. This is not a game. This is serious business. Wishing won't get us there. Unlike what most teach, we do have a part in all of this. Reread Jesus' own words above. Personally I put my trust in what Jesus tells me more than what some men tell me from our modern church. Jesus expects us to read our Bibles, obey His commands, and love him. We need to read God's Word and spend time in prayer. Heaven is too glorious a "hope" to be flippant about.

Chapter and verse numbers were added long after they were written, but we can be assured that God was as much in control of them as the words themselves. God is big on numbers. If seven is perfection, then fourteen must be double perfection, or divine perfection. John 14 is God's divinely perfect plan. It takes only three minutes to read in its entirety, but all we need to know is in it. Please read it all yourself today. Jesus is right now preparing a special place for us, and if we love Him, trust Him, and obey Him, He will come and get us and we will live there with Him for eternity.

Heaven is real. So is hell. If you haven't made your choice, do it now. Putting it off is a decision, and it is the wrong one. God advises us to *"Choose life."* Deuteronomy 30:19.

An Important Homonym

Words that have different meanings are plentiful in the English language. Such words as might, long, file, wind, ball, dash, and fast can all mean at least two things. These words are called homonyms, and some may have multiple meanings, such as pound. But English isn't the only language in which these occur. Greek has the same oddities. An interesting one, "apostacia," can mean either "a falling away" or "a spacial departure." Note, that is spacial, not special.

The importance of the two meanings for apostacia can become monumental when we read 2 Thessalonians 2:3. The verse is a critical "end time" verse that deals with the second coming of Jesus Christ. Let's first read the King James Version:

*"Let no man deceive you by any means; for that day shall not come, except there come a **falling away** first, and that man of sin be revealed, the son of perdition,"*

Did you catch the words, falling away? In the original those words were the word, apostacia. In a more modern translation, the NIV, falling away has been upgraded to the word, rebellion. We are being told here, and rightfully so, that there will be a falling away or a rebellion against Christ and the Father prior to the appearance of the antichrist. None of us can doubt that. In fact, we can already see it taking place, even in America, the nation that was once the bastion of Christianity.

President Obama said in a speech in Turkey that America was not a Christian nation, and most Christians, including me, were appalled. But the more I have thought about it, maybe he was right. Sure, more people claim to be Christian than any other religion in the United States. But if we ask most of them to talk about it, the majority truly have no clue of what it means. We will hear things like, "I believe Jesus was right that we should feed the poor," or "Jesus was a good man," or "I really believe Jesus actually lived."

And even within some of our traditional churches we can find ministers preaching that the resurrection really didn't occur, or that the Bible truly is not "God's Word" to mankind, or that because Jesus died on the cross everyone in the whole world will go to heaven, no matter what. We even now have homosexual ministers and bishops, as well as ministers and church leaders that vote for baby killing.

Even the nation as a whole is trying to kick Jesus and the Father right out of our country. Such things as taking the Bible and prayer out of schools, and the ten commandments out of public buildings, are prime examples. The final straw will be the abandonment by America of God's chosen people, Israel. Yes indeed, a falling away, a rebellion, is occurring. And it will speed up even faster in the months to come. Don't be surprised. God told us it would happen.

But let's get back to the Greek homonym, apostacia. Jerome translated apostacia in the Vulgate into the Latin "discecto," meaning "a spacial departure." Somehow, between the earlier Vulgate and the King James Version the meaning was changed to a falling away. So let's read the King James Version, using what obviously was the earlier interpretation,

"Let no man deceive you by any means; for that day shall not come, except there come a **spacial departure** *first, and that man of sin be revealed, the son of perdition,"*

What could a "spacial departure" be except the rapture? In the first letter to the Thessalonians, chapter 4:16-17, God had written, *"For the Lord Himself will come down from heaven, with a loud command, with the voice of the archangel and with the trumpet call of God, and the dead will rise first. After that, we who are still alive and are left will be caught up together with them in the clouds to meet the Lord in the air. And so we will be with the Lord forever."*

So, which interpretation of apostacia is correct. I believe they both are. Just as God often prophesied two separate events with one prophecy, He did the same thing with the word, apostacia. He told us that we would experience the falling away that we are now seeing, but with the same word he told us that some of us would be a part of the glorious rapture of the true bride of Christ.

Yes, God used the Greek homonym, apostacia for a reason, and we need to understand both meanings. God is complex. So, too, is His Word. But the more we search out the matter, as He wants us to do, the more comfort and peace we gain. He communicated with us thoroughly. He gave us everything we need to know. It is up to us to "search out the matter."

Famous Last Words

People are always intrigued by "famous last words". They are often quite revealing. One writer who was an atheist said it all when his dying words were, "I am as good as without hope, a sad old man gazing into the final chasm."

Compare those chilling words to the glorious final words of evangelist D.L. Moody, "Earth recedes! Heaven opens before me. This is no dream...It is beautiful! It is like a trance! If this is death, it is sweet! God is calling me, and I must go."

Intriguing to me are the last words of Saint Augustine, who wrote so very much that is still studied and loved to this day by Christians around the world. In fact, I am currently rereading his Confessions, and it was written about 400 AD. When Augustine was on his death bed, he actually died for several minutes. Then he miraculously opened his eyes one last time and said to those standing at his bedside, "I have seen Jesus. All that I have written is as straw." He was telling us that nothing he had written came close to experiencing the true glory of Jesus.

The question isn't whether we, or our loved ones or friends, will die. It isn't a question of when, or from what physical cause, or in what manner. The question is which view of eternity they will have open up to them in those moments.

And that begs one more question, "which of our loved ones and friends will we take with us?"

Jesus as a Boy

So often our spiritual eyes are not open when we read our Bibles. We read the surface text and don't stop to ask ourselves, or the Holy Spirit, if there is something else God is saying. Such has always been the case with the story about Jesus as a boy. We are all familiar with the story about Mary and Joseph taking the young Jesus to Jerusalem for the Feast of the Passover, but let's read part of it again with spiritually open eyes:

"After the Feast was over, while His parents were returning home, the boy Jesus stayed behind in Jerusalem, but they were unaware of it. Thinking He was in their company, they traveled on for a day. Then they began looking for Him among their relatives and friends. When they did not find Him, they went back to Jerusalem to look for Him. After three days they found Him in the Temple Courts," Luke 2:41-46.

Often we have talked about a day being the equivalent of a thousand years in the Bible. So, for me, the "day" word automatically triggers my spiritual eyes to open up and start focusing. And what can we see in this little story that no one else may have ever seen?

We look at Abraham as father of the Hebrew nation. For about a thousand years after Abraham the Jews didn't seem miss having a king, even though the other nations around them had one. *"They were unaware of it,"* as we read above.

But when that thousand years was up, they missed having a king. That was about a thousand B.C. Could it be that they will finally find their true King three thousand years later. That would bring us up to about now.

After three days they found Him in the Temple Courts," Luke 2:46.

Shirley's Phenomenal Story

I had a conversation with a wonderful lady named Shirley who is a nurse I know here in Greenville, S.C. What she related has given me several things to muse. It will you, too. Rather than expounding on them, though, I will just tell you Shirley's story and let you mentally explore it for yourself.

Her adult son was in a terrible automobile accident in Florida in which he was hit head on by a drunk driver. Shirley's son was in ICU for over three weeks in a coma and in very bad condition, near death. To set the stage for what happened you need to be aware that although he said he was a Christian, he had never been a church attender and had never even opened a Bible.

Suddenly, while still in the coma, Shirley's son started quoting entire passages of Isaiah, which was most astonishing because, as I said, he knew nothing at all about the Bible. Shirley's daughter ran to the hospital chapel and got a Bible to see if what he was quoting was correct. Amazingly, it was word for word. Then he quoted, "By His stripes you were healed," and immediately opened his eyes.

Once out of the coma, Shirley's son described what had happened. He said he was in a long tunnel that had a glorious light at the end. He expounded on how wonderful and loving the light was. There were two lines of people in the tunnel. One line was moving very fast and was filled with people, all very joyful and singing praise songs to Jesus as they marched by.

The line the son was in was moving very slowly, and he never got to the end of the line to the light. While in the line he was given scriptures, which were the verses he was saying out loud to the people around his bed in the hospital room. Then he was told, "By His stripes you were healed," and immediately he awoke from the coma.

Wisdom

It is ironic that the possibility exists that the most well known Biblical verse in the world may have been erroneously translated into our English language when the King James Bible first came to print in 1611, and the mistake has not been corrected to this day. The scripture I am referring to is one that almost anyone who has ever heard of the Bible can recite, *"In the beginning God created the heavens and the earth."* Genesis 1:1.

The problem actually stems back to St. Jerome's fourth century Latin Vulgate, as well as even the earlier Greek Septuagint that came on the scene in 1 BC. The phrase in question is the very first one in the Bible, *"In the beginning...,"* for although the original Hebrew word, "Be'reasheet," could possibly mean "in the beginning of." It is not possible for it to mean "in the beginning" without the "of." Since there was no object in that sentence for the preposition "of," the translators just dropped it.

In reality, however, be'reasheet is a compound word with the "be" more literally meaning "with," and reasheet meaning "first wisdom." The more accurate translation, therefore, is the one used in the 2100 year old Jerusalem translation into Aramic. That older version of God's Word reads, *"With wisdom God created the heavens and the earth."*

That subtle difference points us to the true original building block of everything, God's wisdom. And that thought was emphasized later in the Bible in Psalm 104:24, *"How many are your works, O Lord! In wisdom you made them all."*

Later, the wisest of all, God, instructed the wisest human of all, Solomon, to strongly advise us in Proverbs 1-4 to seek wisdom. Phenomenally, you and I can not only seek wisdom, but we can receive it, for God graciously gave us the two sources of perfect, divine wisdom. The first of those easy to access sources is the ever exciting Bible, God's true words for mankind. Our second source is prayer, our 24 hour a day direct line to the personification of all wisdom, our awesome heavenly Father. In fact, God's Holy Word says, *"If any of you lacks wisdom, he should ask God, who gives generously to all without finding fault, and it will be given to him. But when he asks, he must believe and not doubt."* James 1:5-6.

The Bible and prayer, our two doorways to true wisdom, for as we just learned, *"With wisdom God created the heavens and the earth."* Genesis 1:1.

December 9, 1917

God had Isaiah prophesy to Israel over and over that if they would not return to Him, judgement would come. Isaiah even predicted in chapter 39 that Israel would be taken over by the Babylonians and the nation would go into exile.

Finally, King Manasseh had heard enough warnings and bad news from Isaiah, so he had him killed in 680 BC. Obviously this murder of His servant Isaiah was an abomination to the Lord. God would not let such an act go unpunished, and Israel was indeed taken captive by the Babylonians. But God foretold when Israel would finally be freed, and how He prophesied it is utterly fascinating.

Over a hundred years after the abomination of the murder of Isaiah, we find the angel Gabriel telling Daniel,

*"From the time... the abomination is set up,... there shall be a thousand two hundred and ninety days. **Blessed** is he who waits and comes to the thousand three hundred and thirty five days."* Daniel 11:11-12 (KJV).

Notice the word *"blessed"* in that scripture because it will be very important to us in a moment.

We know that God often predicts more than one event with one scripture, and that is the case with the above passage, even though it is primarily thought of as a Tribulation prophecy.

I wondered for years about those two numbers in

158

those verses. None of the explanations I read satisfied me. So one night some years back I decided to pray about them.

After praying, I had a strange *nudge* and felt that I should add both of those numbers that Gabriel gave Daniel. I did feel that days here actually referred to years. So 1,290 plus 1,335 gives us a total of 2,625 years.

The next step would be to subtract 680, the BC date of Isaiah's murder, an abomination that could be the starting point for the prophecy. This would get us into AD years. So, when we subtract the 680 from the total of 2,625 years, we get 1945 AD years. Because those 1945 years are Jewish years of only 360 days each, we need to convert them to our years. The final answer is the year 1917 on our calender. The idea, then, is to see if God did anything unusual to *bless* Israel in 1917.

But what about an exact date in 1917? Can we pinpoint an actual date to examine for a massive blessing? Let's jump to the book of Haggai where we find that God is crystal clear that the actual date that Israel would be *blessed*, the date He would make Israel his signet ring, would be the twenty fourth day of the Jewish ninth month:

*"From this day, from this twenty fourth day of the ninth month, give careful thought to the day when the foundation of the Lord's temple was laid....From this day on I will **bless** you....I will shatter the power of foreign kingdoms... On that day... I will make you like my signet ring, for I have chosen you,' declares the Lord Almighty."* Haggai 2:18-23.

Did you notice that God said that on the twenty fourth day of the ninth month He would bless Israel? That date on our calender in 1917 was December 9. So, what happened on that particular date?

On December 9, 1917, British General Alanby, after routing the Turkish army from what was then known as Palestine, surprisingly dismounted from his horse as he approached the Joppa Gate of Jerusalem. As he got off his horse, Alanby said, "I will walk into Jerusalem as a pilgrim and not ride in as a conqueror."

That was the first day since the Babylonians took over Jerusalem that the city was not under enemy occupation. It was the first year in 2,625 Jewish years since the abomination of Isaiah's murder, and it was the actual date that God said He would bless the Hebrew people. Additionally, of course, this led to the rebirth of Israel as a sovereign nation and its own eventual control once again of the Jewish holy city, Jerusalem.

Astounding! Not only did God predict in Daniel exactly to the day when Jesus would ride into Jerusalem as the Messiah, we can also see now that He also predicted in Daniel and Haggai the exact year and date that Israel's enemies would finally be driven out of Jerusalem, December 9, 1917.

Nothing is as astounding as the Word of God. Nothing is as astounding as our God.

Choir Practice

I first read a report by Kelsey Tyler that has haunted me all these years. And since then, I have examined every report and old newspaper account that I could find of the incident, including the first hand article filed by Luke Nichols, the reporter for the local paper, *The Daily Sun*. With each detail I uncovered I became more amazed. Quite frankly, what occurred that night may have had more impact on my thinking than virtually anything that has happened to me personally.

Evidently that March night in 1950 was cold in Beatrice, Nebraska. As usual, choir practice was at 7:30 that Wednesday night, and since this practice was the last one before the Easter Cantata, everyone knew that they needed to be there early so that the actual singing could begin right on time. The Choir director, Martha Paul, had made doubly sure of that. Martha had never been late herself, always getting to the church fifteen minutes early. She had routinely insisted that the choir members arrive no later that 7:25, but this week she was abnormally insistent.

Martha's nineteen year old daughter, Marilyn, was the pianist for the West Side Baptist Church. She was a vivacious but no nonsense young woman who, although she already had a steady job, still lived at home with Martha. That evening Marilyn decided to take a little nap after dinner, so Martha went to her room at 6:45 to wake her up. That gave them thirty minutes to get ready and get to the church. At seven, however, Marilyn had not come downstairs so Martha was getting a little agitated. When she went back to Marilyn's room she was actually furious to find that Marilyn had gone back to sleep. The same thing happened over and over until Martha realized it was 7:25. It was then that the lights went out in the house.

Rowena Vandegrift and her sister were starting to get butterflies in their stomachs. The teenage sisters, along with a friend, had formed The West Side Girls Trio. And this Cantata was to be their coming out debut. They had a solo part in the Cantata this year and tonight was the only time they would actually practice with the choir before the big day. Rowena had some car problems that day, but their friend was picking the sisters up. Unfortunately she was having a problem of her own, with a geometry assignment, and was running a touch behind schedule. Then the lights went out.

Across town, Theodore Charles took his two sons to dinner at Margaret McKinter's home at six that evening. Anne, his wife, was out of town for the night and Margaret had offered to cook corned beef with biscuits and gravy, plus home made apple pie, before Theodore went to choir practice. The boys would just have to be quiet little angels during the rehearsal so that Martha Paul would not be distracted.

Theodore planned to leave Margaret's home at seven, but she was in an especially talkative mood that evening and time slipped by. Then the lights went out.

Gina Hicks was to be another soloist on Sunday,

and she was ready. Choir was the highlight of her week. For some reason, however, her mother, Norma Hicks, was upset about all she had to do to get ready for the next evenings Ladies' Missionary Group that was being held at their house. Finally, after a few words, Gina said she would stay home and help with all the preparation. As to her solo, she knew she was as prepared as she would ever be, so she called her friend, Agnes O'Shaugnessy, and asked her to tell Martha about her change in plans.

When Agnes got the call from Gina, Mary Jones, who she always car pooled with to the church, came to the door. Agnes had gotten a little absorbed in the TV program, "This Is Your Life," so she motioned for Mary to take a seat for a minute or two. Although, they both knew that 7:25 was the absolute latest Martha wanted them to arrive, this show was different, and they sat there until the program ended at 7:27, and the power went off.

It was the pastor's duty to be at the church before anyone arrived, and he had never disappointed. This evening, though, was a crisis. Just as he and his wife and six year old daughter, Susan, were to head over to the church, little Susan had a mishap and spilled punch all down the front of her white pinafore dress and onto the beige rug.

Herb Kipf, a twenty nine year old bachelor, like Marilyn Paul, and Gina Hicks, lived with his parents. He had been with the choir since he was twelve years old. In fact, the church was his life. Although a full time machinist, he had something to do at the church every single day of the week. It was a little after seven, Herb had finished dinner and was working on a letter from the West Side Baptist Church to the secretary of another Baptist church on the other side of town. It took a few minutes longer than he anticipated to compose his thoughts, but at 7:25 he sealed and stamped the letter and headed to his car.

As he was starting to back out the driveway his mother came rushing out the front door, motioning him to roll down his window. "Herb," she almost screamed, "Gladys just called and it's the church. It blew up! just a minute ago, at 7:27."

Herb raced to the church to find it completely gone. He knew he was late. Martha was insistent. Everyone was to be in their places by 7:25 at the very latest. Tears streamed down his face. All his friends? Were they all dead?

The fire truck was already there. Beside it, sobbing, was Martha. He ran to her and they embraced. "Marilyn just wouldn't wake up. She wouldn't wake up."

The fire captain was there. "How many survived?" Herb asked him.

"None," he said. "No one could have survived that blast. Look for yourself. There's nothing there. It was a gigantic gas leak explosion."

A crowd was gathering.

"Martha, was anyone else late?" Herb whispered through his tears.

"I don't know. Let's walk around and find out."

It was then that the miracle was known. Seventeen adults and three children were suppose to have been in that building before 7:27 that March 1, 1950, but not one soul was there. The chances of that happening at the West Side Baptist Church in Beatrice, Nebraska, at Wednesday night choir practice four days before the Easter Cantata are completely incalculable. Never in anyone's memory had there ever been more than three people late the same night. But that night, God was in charge.

And it was then, as the choir was hugging and crying and thankful beyond belief, that Erma Rimrock, a retired woman who had been a member of the church for over forty years, walked into their circle sobbing, "Last week my brother and I purchased the closed down Methodist Church down the street as an investment. We can hold services there as long as you want. And with some cleaning, we should be able to start there this Sunday with the Easter Cantata."

The Two Parachutes

There is a story about two men who were both given parachutes as they were boarding a plane. The first one was told that he would need it if the plane crashed. The second was told that it would make his flight more comfortable. As the flight progressed, both found their parachutes to be far from comfortable. Neither could lie back and rest with it, and the other passengers kept making fun of them and ridiculing them. Finally, the second man threw his to the floor, saying, "This thing is no good. I was lied to." The first man, of course, kept his on, having been told what it was really for. An hour later the airplane lost power. Man number one was saved, and all others aboard perished.

The parachute obviously represents Christianity. Some of us hold on to it because we know that it is the hope for eternal life. Others discard it along their walk because they find out that the promises they were given about it did not come to fruition. They had been led to believe that by becoming Christians their lives on this earth would be much more comfortable. God would take their troubles away from them. He would heal broken relationships supernaturally, eliminate any money concerns, heal all their sicknesses, and make life rosy. When it doesn't happen like that, and their focus is not on the true hope of heaven, many lose heart and lay down their parachutes.

I strongly believe that we should be learning from

the old saints who lived in the Age of Missions (1730 to 1900) who Jesus wrote to in His letter of praise to the Church of Philadelphia in Revelation 3:7-13, rather than learning from the teaching of much of the modern age church that was written to by Jesus in His letter to Laodicia, in which He said, *"I am about to spit you out of my mouth."* Revelation 3:16.

Lately I have been reading a lot from those people of God from the seventeen and eighteen hundreds. Compared to today's church leaders, they spent a lot more time talking about sin and the ongoing need to repent, which means actually turning away from the sin and not just asking God to forgive and then continuing on sinning. But what has really jumped out at me is that they also talked a whole lot more about the hope of heaven, and much, much less about God making their lives a walk through the tulips here on earth.

Yes, God does answer prayers. But the longer we walk with our Lord the more we realize that He does not always give us what we want. He knows what we truly need that will prepare us for the eternal life, and often it is far different from what we are hoping for. Relationships are not always restored supernaturally. Money may still be a struggle (although faithful tithing does result in our basic needs being met). All sicknesses are not taken away, no matter how much faith we may have. Even the apostles were not promised that life would be a rose garden, and not only did they live lives of deprivation, but all except John died horrible deaths.

Jesus told us in John 16:33, *"In this world you will*

have trouble." He did not say we "might," He said we **"will"** have trouble. But He went on to say *"But take heart! I have overcome the world."* He has overcome the world, and as long as we keep our parachutes on we will get to witness that fact first hand. That is our true hope.

We will have troubles. That is a given. *"In fact, everyone who wants to live a godly life in Christ Jesus **will** be persecuted."* 2 Timothy 3:12. If nothing else, the other passengers will make fun of our parachute and ridicule us. God said it would happen, so be prepared. But this world will crash, and the parachute of Christ Jesus will save us. That is our true hope and blessed assurance.

Definitely, Jesus walks right beside us on our daily journey. He is as close as the tear drops on our pillow. And I can attest that He has worked so many phenomenal miracles in my life that have left me awe struck that I have lost count. But these miracles and answered prayers that you and I have, and will continue to receive, are plusses. The main reason for us to put on the parachute is for the crash that will assuredly come when we die or when God puts a stop to the evil downward spiral of this world. So long as we keep heaven as our daily focus, everything else will lose its overwhelming importance and we will be able to retain that unspeakable joy in our lives that is beyond description. Our citizenship is in heaven. We are just experiencing a very brief journey to get there. Heaven is our true home.

One final thought. The thirteenth century Jewish Rabbi and philosopher, Nahmanides, said "the degree of

Divine direction to an individual person depends on that person's individual choice of how close to God he or she wishes to be." This deep truth was stated a little differently fifty years earlier by Maimonides, whose works are now considered a cornerstone for Jewish thought. Maimonides wrote, "Only the totally righteous have one-on-one Divine direction, and even that guidance may not ensure a life free of pain and suffering. For the rest of us, chance and accidents do occur. It's our choice as to where we, as individuals, fall within that spectrum of behavior that stretches from intimate Divine direction to total random chance." We can choose to stay close to God with our parachute tightly buckled or not. The choice is ours.

With our focus being on Jesus and the heavenly home He secured for us, we will finish the race that Paul talked about. Then we will personally witness what he alluded to in 1 Corinthians 2:9, *"No eye has seen, no ear has heard, no mind has conceived what God has prepared for those who love Him."* While we await that heavenly joy, we should stay as close to God as we can, through prayer and Bible study, so that we might realize the Divine direction we so need and desire on our path that will take us there. With Jesus beside us, and our eyes fixed intently on our heavenly home, we can have joy both during the troubles of this earthly world and in the glorious, tear free lives we will experience in the true everlasting world we have yet to see.

Be Thankful

The only place I have found in the Bible that actually tells us "God's will for our lives" says, *"Be joyful always, pray continually. and be thankful in all situations, for that is God's will for your life in Christ Jesus."* 1 Thessalonians 5:16-18.

The third part, being thankful, destroys every negative attitude. I recently heard that a university study proved that it is impossible to think of two things at the same time. I'm amazed they needed a study to prove that, but at any rate, it points to the fact that if we are thinking a thankful thought, it is literally impossible to think something bad.

If we obey God's will for us, it will cure every emotional ill in our lives. The next time we are distraught about anything at all, we need to start thinking of things we are thankful for, and then thank God for them. Life probably would be a whole lot more pleasant if we just paid closer attention to the manual for life God has given us, His Holy Word.

Blue Eyed Paul

There use to be a section in *Readers Digest* called, "My Most Unforgettable Character." I'm not sure, it may still be one of the features. If so, were I ever asked to submit a piece on my most unforgettable character, it would be a short one. Mainly because I didn't know him very long. But "unforgettable" would definitely be one word that could be used to describe him. Allow me to explain.

About fifteen years ago I was invited to visit an evening service at a small church in Orlando, Florida. Upon finding the location of the address I was given, I found that it was meeting in an almost abandoned strip center. I got there a little early, and there were some people inside praying for the upcoming service. I decided to wait outside until closer to the starting time.

While I was standing a few doors down from the church, I noticed a man walking across the six lane boulevard in front of the strip center. Interestingly, he was walking directly to me. When he got close I had a sense that he was an extremely nice person. You know how we sometimes get those "vibes" right away? At any rate, I felt drawn to him immediately. I'd say he was about 55 or 60 years old, fairly tall, clean, pleasant looking, with the bluest eyes I had ever seen. I couldn't take my eyes off those blue eyes. They were penetrating, but extremely friendly. Don't take this wrong, but they were almost loving.

We struck up a conversation and I found out that his name was Paul, and he was a carpenter. He was on his way to Miami to do some construction work. I really liked the man, a lot. Of course, God was on my mind so we talked about that a little. Then he said he had to go. For some strange reason I handed him ten dollars of the fifteen I had in my pocket. He had in no way asked for any money. And in fact, we had not discussed money at all. But he didn't refuse me. He thanked me very much, then said, "God bless you," in the most sincere manner I had ever heard, and he walked away.

Words fail to describe the peace that almost flooded my body as I watched Paul walking away. It was surreal. And his "God bless you" was somehow said in a way that still echoes in my mind to this day.

As I watched Paul walking across the street, this blue eyed stranger vanished before my very eyes.

"Do not forget to entertain strangers, for by so doing some people have entertained angels without knowing it." Hebrews 13:2.

One Kingdom

Whether you live in Australia, Brazil, Slovakia, New Zealand, Vietnam, Mexico, Belize, United States, Zimbabwe, Germany, France, South Africa, or Canada, you share one thing with every other reader. You have national pride. We all have it. Some stronger than others, but we all have it. If we perceive our own nation changing, or turning away from the things we love about her, we find it extremely disturbing. We all share that, too.

In that light, though, the Lord has really been working on me in the last little while, and the result for me has been fantastic. Lately, a new idea has crystallized in my mind that should have been so obvious, but for some reason has always been obscured. Therefore, I will endeavor to explain a radical change in my thinking that you, too, might find refreshing.

As I said, we all probably occasionally see changes made in our own nations that bother us a lot. As a conservative Christian American I personally have been experiencing that quite a bit lately. Being a child of the 40's my views of what the United States should be like are firmly ingrained, and the rapid departure from that image of late has both saddened me and even occasionally filled me with pure anger. Since so much is happening so quickly on a global scale, you may have experienced the same feelings about your nation.

In studying the book of Jeremiah we find that God directs the prophet in things concerning the Babylonian captivity, but in so doing, God also talks to us about the upcoming end times period, the following Millennial Kingdom, and heaven. While digging into these scriptures some verses jumped up at me and gave me a whole new view of everything in our lives today that has radically changed my emotions about what is going on around us. Let's look first at one thing God said to the nation of Israel:

"Though I completely destroy all the nations among which I scatter you, I will not completely destroy you." Jeremiah 30:11.

Since God has not destroyed as of yet all of the nations in which the Jews have been scattered, this prophecy obviously deals with a future time. And although most books talk about the Jews having been scattered throughout seventy nations, I think we can agree that in reality there were at least a few Jews in every single nation on earth before the ingathering began in 1948. Therefore, at some point in the future, God will destroy every single nation on earth, except for Israel. At some point, Germany, Belize, Japan, United States, Slovakia, Australia, and every other nation listed above will cease to exist. In fact, no nation but Israel will exist at some time in the future. Actually, let's read further:

"This is what the Lord says,
he who appoints the sun to shine by day,
who decrees the moon and stars to shine by night,
who stirs up the seas so that the waves roar -
the Lord Almighty is his name:

'Only if these decrees vanish from my sight'
declares the Lord
'will the descendants of Israel
ever cease to be a nation before me." Jeremiah
31:35-36.

It makes so much sense if we ponder it. When Jesus returns, he will reign over the whole world from Jerusalem for the next thousand years. We all know that. His reign will be that of King. We are told that people will live in towns and cities all over the world during that time, but it would be ludicrous for us to imagine that these towns and cities would be parceled into national boundaries like they are now. Jesus will be King of it all. It will be a kingdom. One kingdom. And it will be called Israel, which literally means, "who strives with God."

For me, an American, to get myself in a big dither about the US changing is ridiculous. The United States is not an eternal entity. It is destined to be completely dissolved anyway. Only God's Kingdom is eternal. And after all, that is where my citizenship lies. The same is true of your country and your citizenship. We read, *"But our citizenship is in heaven. And we eagerly await our Savior from there, the Lord Jesus Christ."* Philippians 3:19-20.

Yes, the whole world is changing. The Bible tells us that a global world government is coming, even before the Lord returns. Then when He returns and takes His throne in Jerusalem, there will be one world, one nation, one Kingdom. It will be called Israel, and its citizens will be those of us "who strive with the Lord."

So, like me, calm what is churning in your belly about your nation and this world. Our true citizenship nation is truly glorious, unchanging, and everlasting. We can let our "national pride" soar to the heavens. We are but witnesses of this changing world. Our true nation will never let us down or disappoint us. Our true citizenship is in the everlasting Kingdom of Christ Jesus.

Indescribable Love

Imagine with me a for a moment being Jesus, and knowing how unbelievably great was His Father's love for Him. It's no wonder Jesus could trust Him so much in every aspect of His life. We can understand how Jesus walked through every situation of His life in complete confidence, knowing how much God loved Him. Who wouldn't be so calm about life if he knew that God the Father loved him as much as He loved Jesus, His only begotten son? Oh, how wonderful that would be. Our lives would be drastically different if we had that knowledge, but obviously we don't deserve to be on the same level as Jesus when it comes to God's love.

Here is where I am going to startle you, and if you will truly accept and absorb the truth I am going to impart, I am going to change your life forever.

If you are truly a believer in Christ, God does love you **exactly the same** as He loves Jesus.

"That's not possible," you say.

Every Christian has certainly read the 17th chapter of John, but 999 out of 1,000 who have read it have missed the greatest gem in the Bible. That chapter, of course, is the last prayer that Jesus prayed before he was arrested. In that prayer He prayed for Himself, then He prayed for His disciples, then He prayed for *"those who will believe in me through their message."* John 17:20.

If you are a Christian, that is you. In that prayer, Jesus says His Father, *"hast loved **them**, as thou hast* *loved me."* John 17:23 (KJV).

That "**them**" is you, and that "**as**" means "**the same as**". Get that in your mind and spirit. God the Father loves you <u>the very same</u> as He loves Jesus. No wonder our Lord could tell you so emphatically not to be anxious or troubled about anything. God loves you **as much as** He loves Jesus. Christ said it, and He does not lie. With that fact firmly implanted in your soul, this day should surely be the beginning of an entirely new and joyous life. How could it be otherwise?

God loves you with the <u>exact same amount of love</u> with which He loves Jesus.

Understanding

Recently I was reading a grand old work of fiction printed in 1948 called <u>The Big Fisherman</u>, written by the fabulous author, Lloyd C. Douglas, who also wrote such books as <u>Magnificent Obsession</u> and <u>The Robe</u>.

The Big Fisherman is a fast paced book with fictitious characters whose lives intermingle with the lives of Biblical characters, including Peter, the inspiration for the title. At any rate, what caught my attention was a fictional discussion by the disciples while Jesus was not present. In it, they are saying that Jesus was asking them to go to a town and they didn't understand why. Bartholomew declares that, "Jesus is teaching them to have faith." Thomas then says, "But - can't a man have faith - and understanding, too?" That is when the lightning bolt hit me, for Bartholomew replies, "No, that's what faith is for! It's for when we can't understand." And Peter adds, "That's true, when a man understands, he doesn't need any faith."

We all know that, of course, but for some reason it jumped out at me in a way it never had before. It reminded me of the true incident that occurred some years back when a good believer traveled to India for the sole purpose of having Mother Teresa pray for him that God would give him clarity in his life. When she heard the request her reply was an instantaneous "No".

The man was stunned and said, "But Mother Teresa, you have always had clarity."

To this she laughed and gently said, "No, I have never had clarity, I have only had trust. I will pray for God to give you trust"

So, if you have been looking for understanding, or clarity, about how or when God will answer your situation or do this or that, stop thinking about it. It probably is time for absolute, unquestioning faith. It is time to sit back and calmly trust. In God's eyes we are worth much more than the sparrows. Just remember, *"In all things God works for good for those who love Him."* That is all we need to know.

333rd Prophecy Discovered

When I saw it I trembled. And it seemed as if only by accident that it happened. I stumbled across something that sent chills up and down my spine. Whether it was a "stumble upon" or a "revelation from on high" I can not say, but it is definitely the most important thing that has ever come to me.

In my book, <u>Unlocking God's Secrets,</u> I included the 332 prophecies that were fulfilled in the life of Jesus. As I was listing those 332 prophecies for that book I wondered why God did not have 333 prophecies. He obviously uses numbers for added meaning in so many things that He does. And just as doubling a number gives it emphasis like adding "er" to a word makes it "more," the tripling of a number is like changing the "er" to "est" makes it the most, such as strong, stronger, strongest. Thus we have "verily, verily" meaning "double truth" and 666 (6 being the number for man) describing the antichrist, the very worst of mankind's traits, as in, *"The mind of man is the enemy of God."* Romans 8:7. At any rate, I felt that it would have made sense for God to have had 333 prophecies of Jesus since 3 is a divine number dealing with God and the Holy Trinity.

I can now declare emphatically that God did include the 333rd prophecy of Jesus in His Holy Word, and it is the most phenomenal of them all. It is in the 333rd prophecy that the name of the Messiah was foretold to be Jesus. That's right, God prophesied the name of Jesus.

And God foretold it 520 years before Jesus was born.

Go with me to the book of Zechariah in which God is talking to Zechariah and says,

*"Take the silver and the gold and make a crown, and set it on the head of the high priest, **Joshua** son of Jehozadak. Tell him this is what the Lord Almighty says, 'Here is the **man whose name** is the Branch, and he will branch out from his place and build the temple of the Lord. It is he who will build the temple of the Lord, and he **will be clothed with majesty and will sit and rule on his throne. And he will be a priest on his throne. And there will be harmony between the two**."* Zechariah 6:11-13.

First we need to understand that Joshua, Yeshua, and Jesus are all three the same name. They mean "Salvation" or "the Lord is Salvation." So in the above verses God is saying *"Here is the man whose name* (Joshua, Yeshua, Jesus) *will be clothed with majesty and will sit and rule on his throne. And he will be a priest on his throne."*

God foretold in this verse the exact name of the coming Messiah. God told the world that the Savior's name would be Jesus. Can you grasp the magnitude of that? And not until now, in these end times, was this wondrous prophecy made known to us. Wow!!

God went on to say in the above verse, *"And there will be harmony between the two."* That is extremely important because Jesus is the first to be both king and high priest. Even Moses could not fulfill both offices, as his brother, Aaron, was high priest while Moses ruled.

There is much that could be discussed about these incredible verses, but the most important thing obviously is that God the Father foretold that his Son's name would be Jesus.

And by the way, the name Jehozadak, the father of the Joshua (Jesus) in that Zechariah verse above, means "The Lord is righteous."

Yes, our Lord God is righteous, and he is the Father of the One who would be our salvation, Jesus Christ. And he foretold his Son's name in plain sight for those of us in these end days to "stumble across."

Talk about an exciting nugget. WOW!

We now know the 333rd prophesy of the Messiah. **His name will be Jesus**.

Praise His Holy Name.

Myrrh

The Bible is so intricately woven that oftentimes in order to find what God is talking about we need to look at the threads that a word, a phrase, or a thought weave throughout the entire 66 books. An example is the word, Myrrh.

Myrrh is an aromatic gum resin that was used to cover bodies for burial in Biblical times. It is actually mentioned four times in the New testament.

The first time, of course was in Matthew when it was given to the baby Jesus as a gift by the Magi, along with the gifts of gold and frankincense. What a strange gift for a baby, but it had a meaning. The gold represented Jesus as a king, the frankincense was for the role of Jesus as a priest, and the myrrh pointed to His sacrifice of death for you and me.

We then see Myrrh again in Mark when it was offered to Jesus on his last day in a wine drink, which he refused.

The third instance of myrrh in the New Testament was in the Gospel of John, when we are told that the body of Jesus was covered in myrrh when it was placed in the tomb.

The fourth mention of myrrh is normally missed by most of us. The second church that Jesus writes to in Revelation, Smyrna, the persecuted church, actually meant myrrh.

So we see myrrh at the birth of Jesus, while He was alive, also during His three days in the grave, and again after He had risen and gone to heaven and was writing the letter to Smyrna.

The picture given of Myrrh is of persecution, suffering and death. But the important thing to understand can best be summed up in four of the phrases lifted out of the letter from Jesus to those persecuted saints in Smyrna. Those phrases apply equally to us today. Those four phrases from the lips of Jesus are:

"I know your afflictions and your poverty."

"Do not be afraid of what you are about to suffer."

"Be faithful, even to the point of death, and I will give you the crown of life."

"He who overcomes will not be hurt at all by the second death." Revelation 2:9-11.

A Wrenching Tale

One of the things I learned early in my walk with Jesus was that the more I read about God showing up in miraculous ways in other people's lives, the more it built my own faith. And one of the sources I found for those stories was *Guideposts* magazines. They always did an admirable job of separating truth from fiction, so I devoured those stories within hours of getting their monthly magazine in the mail.

In *Guideposts'* September, 1996, issue a story appeared that truly caught my attention, and got Barb and I involved in a personal way. The lead character was a fellow named Wayne Vanderpoel who lived just north of Tampa, Florida, in a little town of Pinellas Park. Wayne had been an insurance adjuster years earlier who had been introduced to the plight of migrant workers and their deplorable living conditions. Back then these workers were mostly American citizens, but they lived in almost slave conditions. Wayne's heart was touched and he wanted to help.

Christmas day, 1982, crystallized in Wayne's mind that God wanted him to help as well. As *Guideposts* later reported, that special day Wayne got a call from his good friend and pastor, Bill Cruz, who said, "Wayne, we've got sixty migrants just in from Georgia with no place to stay. We put them in an unheated building, and they have no blankets or sleeping bags. The temperature is falling to

190

eighteen degrees tonight. They'll freeze. Can you help?"

Wayne said he didn't know what he could do, but he would try to think of something. So he and his wife, Marie, got on their knees and prayed. An idea came. He would call the local country music station and ask them to put out an appeal. The response he got from the disc jockey who had answered the phone was, "It's Christmas. Nobody's even listening to the radio. They're all celebrating. Nobody will bring you anything."

To that, Wayne stated, "If you put out the appeal, God will do the rest."

Ten or eleven songs were played, and finally the DJ made a short announcement about the need and gave out Wayne's address. Ten or fifteen minutes later a car pulled up at Wayne's house and a lady walked up the drive carrying a blanket. Another person brought two. Within a half an hour cars were lined down the street and around the corner. Marie started putting the blankets in the van, but because of the room the seats took up, the van was quickly filled to the ceiling. There were still four piles of blankets in the yard, and more cars were coming.

Then Marie had an idea, take the seats out of the van. The problem that cropped up immediately was that Wayne needed an eleven-sixteenths-inch socket wrench to unbolt the seats, and Wayne didn't have one. All the neighbors were gone, and of course, the stores were closed. The answer, Wayne and Marie walked into the house, got on their knees and prayed.

I'll let Wayne tell you what he told *Guideposts*:

"About five o'clock a lady drove up and walked down the driveway holding a small grocery bag. She said she had come from Safety Harbor after hearing the broadcast.

'I don't have a blanket, but here are some children's clothes,' she said, thrusting the bag toward me.

I took it and, while thanking her, felt something hard in the bag. I looked in the bag - and pulled out a wrench, eleven sixteenths of an inch to be exact.

I was stupefied. As the woman headed for her car, I called, 'Ma'am, why did you put this wrench in the bag? It's the very thing we needed.'

She looked puzzled. 'What do you mean?'

'We asked for blankets but you brought this. Why?'

'I really don't know,' she said. 'I started out of the house, had to come through the garage and saw it lying on my husband's workbench. He's been dead for four months and it was just where he left it. Migrants work on their cars, I thought, so I scooped it up.'

'When did you leave Safety Harbor?' I asked.

'About forty five minutes ago.'

I looked at my watch. That was just when Marie and I were on our knees asking God for a wrench."

I don't know how many times I read that story. Each time it sent chills up my spine. Finally I picked up the phone and called the information operator. Then I called Mr. Vanderpoel and asked, "did that story about the wrench actually happen?"

Wayne assured me that it did, and that at that moment he was looking at the very wrench, because he had mounted it on his wall as a reminder of what God can do if we only trust

Two days later Barb and I headed from Jupiter, Florida, where we lived at the time, to Pinellas Park. I wanted to see the wrench for myself, and shake Wayne's hand in person. The meeting was lovely, and I soon learned that the wrench was the turning point in Wayne and Marie's lives. They had decided after it happened to work full time in a migrant ministry and since then had relied totally on God. But Wayne laughed as he said that each month was crisis time, although God had never let them down. I asked him to explain and he said it would take days, but he gave me some stories. One was the time they needed exactly $88.75 to pay their electric bill or the power would be turned off the following day. They prayed, and a lady came to the door about an hour later and said that God told her to come to that house and give the man inside $89, so she handed Wayne $89 and walked away.

Needles to say, Barb and I started helping as we could from then on. And there were some funny times. For instance, one time we got an extra $1,000 and wanted to send it to Wayne. When he got the check he called to thank me. His words were, "When I saw the size of the check I told Marie we were in trouble, because something big was about to break." We laughed about that, but sure enough, two days later their air conditioner broke and it cost them $998 to get it fixed.

Since those days, I have been fortunate enough to seek out and become friends with others who have relied totally on God the way Wayne and Marie did. There are more than you might imagine. Dr. Michael Guido, the Sower, comes to mind. He died recently at age 95 and was working, saving souls, right up to the end. In over seventy years in ministry he never asked a man for anything, only making his needs known to his Lord. And his needs were always met, mostly in extremely miraculous ways.

God is real. God is loving. And God is a provider to those who trust and rely on him completely.

Put everything into God's hands, and eventually you will see God's hands in everything. And that includes eleven-sixteenth-inch socket wrenches.

We Can Do Something

Dr. David Jeremiah wrote of a true story about a young girl who was terminally ill. She went to her pastor and asked him what she could do for Jesus in the time she had left. The pastor suggested that she make a list of people in their town who she knew needed Christ. She did, and she prayed often. After the girl died her prayer list was found, under her pillow. It contained fifty six names. All fifty six people had accepted Christ; the last one on the night before her death.

The Jordan Shadows

The thought seems to arise all the time that God was unfair to Moses to not let Moses cross over the Jordan just because of one act of anger. The problem really is that people are not looking at the entire picture of the Bible. They are not realizing that although Old Testament events really did happen, they were <u>all</u> a shadow of things to come. Just as Jesus spoke in parables when he taught the people of His day, the entire Old Testament is a big parable made up of smaller parables, and we need to "search out the matter" to find out what is really being said.

With that in mind, we need to realize that the river Jordan is a "type" or "shadow" of death. The promised land, of course, is a "shadow", or picture, of heaven. Moses was not allowed to cross the river Jordan because he is a "type," or picture of the law, and the law can never defeat death and get people to heaven. No matter how hard we try to obey the Old Covenant laws, we can never defeat death. Only Jesus accomplished that, and only in being covered by His blood can we do it. Jesus is the Way.

The entire story of the Israelites crossing Jordan is one of the most fascinating in the Bible. The person who was allowed to lead the Israelites over was Joshua, whose actual name in Hebrew was Yeshua, the exact same name as Jesus. So Again, following Jesus is the only way to cross over into the promised land.

Interestingly, when we read the awesome story in Joshua, we find other elements, which, if taken for their true meaning make us shudder once again at the magnificence of God's Word. For instance, the Ark of the Covenant, which is again a "type" of Jesus went across the river first. The Ark is a "type" because inside it were three things that symbolize Jesus:

1- the unbroken ten commandments, because He is the only person who did not break a single one;

2- some manna, symbolizing, of course, that Jesus is the "Bread of life;" and,

3- Aaron's staff that budded after it was a dead stick, which is a picture of Christ's resurrection.

Another shadow in this marvelous story of crossing the Jordan is one that I dare say you may have missed. I had read Joshua over and over for years before it hit me. Let's read it.

"Now the Jordan is at flood stage all during harvest. Yet as soon as the priests who carried the ark reached the Jordan and their feet touched the water's edge, the water from upstream stopped flowing. It piled up in a heap a great distance away, at a town called Adam in the vicinity of Zarethan." Joshua 3:15-16.

Did you catch it this time? As soon as the feet of the priests carrying the Ark (Jesus) touched the Jordan, its waters flowing downstream were cut off, and the water stood in a heap all the way back to the town of Adam. That's right, the water flowed back to the town of **Adam**. Any of us should be able to see God's meaning in that.

Jesus would erase the curse of death all the way back to the original curse of Adam.

This allowed the Old Testament saints to get into heaven. This is gigantic. It included all the Jews who had tried to get into heaven by following the law. We can see this truth further in the fact that God instructed the Israelites after they crossed over the then dry Jordan to have one person from each of the twelve tribes go back and pick up twelve stones from the middle of the Jordan, stones that were to represent each of the twelve Jewish tribes, and carry them over to the promised land.

Remember, there were thousands of Old Testament saints who did the best they could to follow God's covenant. They did not have Jesus as their Savior as we do, but the Jordan (death) piling up all the way back to Adam, lets us know that Jesus would make a way for those saints of the Old Testament.

The entire story of the Jordan crossing is one of the most phenomenal stories of salvation in the Bible. In this story, as in all others in the Old Testament, we should concentrate on what God is really saying rather than being human and trying to bring God down to our level by looking at what we perceive to be unfair treatment of Moses. Concentrate always on Jesus, both in reading the entire Bible and in life. Everything is always about Jesus. Everything is His story.

Mystery Tears

As you may know, several years ago I became a hospice volunteer. About that time there was a story going around hospice circles. It was about a volunteer who went to a nursing home for her initial visit with her new patient. When she walked into the room she noticed that a chair was pushed up next to the bed. She made a comment something like, "I'm glad to see you had a visitor here," pointing to the chair.

The old man said, "No, that is where Jesus sits when I talk with Him."

A few days later the volunteer came back but was told by the floor nurse that the old man had just died. She said it was really interesting that when they went into his room an hour or so earlier they found the old man dead, with his head in the chair.

That story really touched me. I could just visualize that old man dying with his head in the lap of Jesus. What a way to go! At any rate, about the same time I heard that story, I was reading a book on prayer by Jill Briscoe. In it she said that she always visualized Jesus sitting at the foot of her bed when she prayed. I started thinking about that, and decided I would start doing something similar to try to improve my own prayer life.

Now, the way I pray every night is to kneel down in front of my living room couch, with my head on a couch pillow. I like to kneel because I feel that I personally am humbled when I approach His throne. At any rate, I decided to place a couch pillow right beside my normal pillow and visualize Jesus there beside me.

The result of adding that pillow beside mine was phenomenal. Can you imagine having Jesus next to you, praying along with you for something. I know that we have knowledge that He is seated at the right hand of God in heaven, and is always interceding for us, but to think that He is literally right beside us when we pray is truly awesome. I mean, ponder it yourself. Imagine kneeling next to Jesus and having Him pray along with you for something. Can you come up with a situation to which the Father would say "no" to Jesus. Visualizing that scenario in my own living room increased my faith that my prayers were being heard and would be answered.

It got to the point that I felt his presence was so strong next to me that I actually at times did visualize Him being there. I know it sounds crazy, and I admit it was just my imagination, but He became so real to me that sometimes I would lean over and kiss His head. My prayer time became a time of loving Jesus, with Him praying right beside me.

Then I started something else. I started sitting on the floor for a time before I knelt and went into prayer. I would just talk to Jesus about what I wanted to pray to the Father about. Only after I got through talking with Him and discussing the situation would I get on my knees and start to pray. I would glance over to my side and almost see Jesus doing the same. It got so realistic that sometimes after I had finished praying I would look over to Jesus and see that He was still praying, so I would bow my head again and pray some more like He was.

At other times I would look over at Him when I started to pray and see Him just looking at me as if to say, "We already prayed about this before. Why do you want to pray again? It has already been taken care of." Then I would remember that, sure enough, we had prayed about that before, so I would just start thanking God that He had answered that prayer, even if the answer had not yet been manifested. By the way, those prayers always were answered the way I had hoped.

The point of me telling you about this is to let you know that I really became much closer to Jesus during that period. And then something truly astounding happened.

All of a sudden one night when I started to pray, tears started streaming down my face. That had happened before, of course, but always before I had been emotional at the moment that it happened. The tears were either tears of joy or tears of sadness when it had happened before.

What was strange this time was that I was neither unusually joyful or sad at the time that these tears started flowing. The tears just came for no reason, and there was no way for me to stop them. Believe me, I did try to stop them. The next night the same thing happened. And it happened again the next night. In fact, it kept happening like that every single night for several weeks.

As soon as I uttered the first word in prayer, the tears would start flowing uncontrollably. And they would not stop until after I had finished praying. I finally started taking a towel with me every time I knelt to pray so that I could continually wipe away the tears. It was so very odd. At times I felt foolish, wiping away the endless flow of tears that ran down my cheeks.

Finally after quite a few weeks I decided to ask Jesus about it. So I said, "Dear Jesus, I don't understand the tears. I am not especially joyful or sad, but they keep rolling down my face. Why is that?"

Then it happened. For the first time in my life I actually heard the voice of God. I don't know if another person in the room would have heard it, but to me it was audible. At the same time, it was like every cell in my body heard it, too. It was indescribable. I have since heard it two other times. And all three times the message was far from anything I would have thought of myself. They were all three very startling statements. And they were all three such that I will never forget a single syllable of what He said.

This time, remember, I had just said, "Dear Jesus, I don't understand the tears. I am not especially joyful or sad, but they keep rolling down my face. Why is that?"

God's voice answered very distinctly, *"Those are My tears, because you are talking with me."*

It was incredible. Never in a million years would I have thought of that as the explanation for those tears. The thought of tears flowing out of my eyes being anyone's but my own would have seemed ludicrous to me. Until, that is, I heard it from God. I will never forget those words as long as I live.

Obviously, God longs for us to really have deep communication with Him. And that can't be done with sporadic, quick prayers. It takes time. A two minute prayer doesn't do it. Sometimes it happens in ten minutes. Sometimes thirty. Sometimes it takes an hour or more. But whatever it takes, it is worth it. And it is what God longs for.

God loves you and me so much more than we could ever imagine. What a phenomenally loving God we have!

We don't realize it, but we evidently bring Jesus unbelievable joy when we truly, intimately, talk with Him.

"Those are My tears," He told me, *"because you are talking with me,"*

He Will Kill You

I once had a hospice patient named Dr. Alfred Smith, who was Billy Graham's very first music director. Dr. Smith had written over fifty hymns in his life, including "*Surely Goodness And Mercy.*" I sat at his feet learning for five months before he died, and I came to love him like a father.

I once asked him what the most awesome miracle he had ever seen was. He told me that in the late 40's he was working with an evangelist named Jack Wirtz in New Jersey. They were holding street meetings at night and often got over 500 people out to hear them. Dr. Smith would sing and draw the crowds, and Jack Wirtz would do the preaching.

There was one woman who was a known communist who came every night and heckled them constantly. One night Jack Wirtz had had enough. He stopped in the middle of his sermon and said to the woman across the crowd, "If you say one more disparaging word about my Lord Jesus, He will kill you."

Dr. Smith told me the woman cackled like a witch, took one step back, and fell over a curb. At that exact moment a car came around the corner and hit her. She was instantly dead.

I was stunned. "I'll bet that stopped the meeting."

Dr. Smith was deep in thought, reliving that incredible event. Finally, "Yes, the meeting stopped while the ambulance came and took her body away. Then Jack started preaching again. This time on the wrath of God. The people listened intently."

Good Samaritan Prophecy

I believe that all the parables that Jesus told are rich with underlying meanings, but most of the time we don't dig much deeper than the surface message that Jesus was trying to convey. In reality, though, I feel strongly that every parable contains prophecy that can be spine tingling to search out.

For instance, we all know that the parable of the Good Samaritan in Luke 10 represents the commandment that Jesus listed as the second most important, to "*love your neighbor as yourself.*" Matthew 22:39. So we read the parable of the Good Samaritan, think of loving our neighbor, and continue on reading Luke 11. We think we have gotten from the story what we were suppose to get.

Unfortunately, we often don't dig deep enough to find the truly exciting underlying types, shadows, and yes, prophecy. When we do, we find that the man who was robbed and left half dead in the story is a picture of Adam or humanity.

The robber, of course, is Satan.

The first person in the story that comes along and steps around the fallen man is a priest. This represents the Law of Moses, which obviously could not save the man. Then a Levite comes by and likewise walks around the man. The Levite represents the sacrifices, which also could not save fallen man.

But then comes the Good Samaritan, which is Jesus Himself.

At this point we see something very unusual and extremely interesting. We see the Good Samaritan (Jesus) pour both oil and wine into the fallen man's wounds. Oil is the Old Testament or Old Covenant representation of the Holy Spirit, while wine is the New Testament or New Covenant representation of the Holy Spirit. The deeper we dig, the more phenomenal we find God's Word to be.

Once the Holy Spirit has been poured into the wounds, the Good Samaritan (Jesus) takes the man to the inn, which represents the church. Here is where the parable becomes prophetic of the Second Coming, because the Good Samaritan (Jesus) leaves the innkeeper two denarii. A denarii was a days wage, and we know that *"With the Lord a day is like a thousand years,"* 2 Peter 3:8. So the church is given two days wage, or two thousand years, until the Good Samaritan (Jesus) returns, at which time He will give the innkeeper (the Church) an unlimited amount of denarii (Eternity).

This two day (two thousand year) prophecy is very consistent with all the other Second Coming prophecies, including the two very obvious ones found in Exodus and Hosea. In the first one the Lord said to Moses, *"Go to the people and consecrate them today and tomorrow. Have them wash their clothes and be ready by the third day, because on that day the Lord will come down on Mount Sinai in the sight of all the people."* Exodus 19:11.

The other one in Hosea 6:2 says, *"After two days He will revive us; on the third day He will restore us, that we may live in His presence."*

Remember, Proverbs 25:2 says, *"It is the glory of God to conceal a matter; to search out a matter is the glory of kings."* The redeemed of Christ will reign with Him in His kingdom, so we are the *"kings"* referred to above who are suppose to search out the things that God has hidden for us in the scriptures. And it really is an exciting treasure hunt. Nothing in life comes close, or is nearly as important.

The point of the prophecy we just uncovered in the parable of the Good Samaritan is that in two thousand years from when He went away, Jesus will return. In the Jewish calender, that time is here. And in the Gentile calender (ours), the time is very close.

Praise God! Look up for our redemption is nigh.

I can hardly wait.

Trust

The word faith is commonplace in Christianity. We are constantly reminded that we should have faith in Christ, faith in the power of prayer, faith in His saving grace, faith for a miracle, faith for this and faith for that. May I submit that if we but trust Him, everything else falls into place.

There is a difference in those two words, and it is huge. We have faith with our heads, but trust comes from the heart. Comparing faith to trust is like comparing a drop of water to the ocean. But unwavering trust is tough. It relies on God not only knowing what is truly best for us, but also loving us so much that He will always give us that best thing, even though it might be extremely painful to us as we go through it. Pure trust understands that in our happiness and in our sadness, everything is inevitably being done for the best, even though we may not even realize it in this life.

Yes, trust can be a hard row to hoe. We would rather have faith that God will bring us through the difficult time we might be facing and allow the answer we desire to be manifested. Although our head may tell us that God can see the future all the way into eternity, and it may even tell us that God loves us as His child, deep within us we would rather the outcomes of each life situation be determined by our own desires than dictated by a second party's will, even if that second party is the all knowing God of everything. To truly trust may be one of the most courageous things in life, even in the life of a committed Christian.

However, trust is achievable. And believe it or not, it is demanded. Jesus commanded, *"Trust in God, trust also in Me."* John 14:1.

In <u>Unlocking God's Secrets</u> we discussed that the word "believe" in our Bibles does not nearly do justice to the original Greek word, "pistevo." A part of the definition of pistevo is: "To trust, with implications of total commitment to the One who is trusted."

The more we thoughtfully search out the matter, the more we find out that Augustus Gordon was totally correct when he answered Brennan Manning's question, "Could you define the Christian life in a single sentence?"

Gordon's response was, "Brennan, I can define it in a single word: trust."

Once we have absolute trust, our entire world changes. Psalm 40:4 says, *"Blessed is the man who makes the Lord his trust."* And how utterly right that statement is. Once complete trust is a part of us, anxiety and stress evaporate. That *"joy that passes all understanding"* becomes a part of our life. Somehow, even the harshest trials we face in this life are not nearly as painful and all consuming when we fully trust our Lord.

But where does this total trust come from. I think it comes from love, our love for Him. As I am beginning to see it, when we love God enough, our desires in our worldly life are lessened in favor of our desire for God's will to be done. It is kind of like a beautiful marriage in which one partner wants his or her spouse's happiness above their own.

A few are fortunate enough to have such love for the Savior the day they first meet Him. For others of us, that love takes time, as the relationship builds, as we learn that the commandment Jesus said was above all others, to *"love God with all of our heart, soul and mind,"* is truly the most important thing in life, as well as being the commandment that makes all of Christian living so easy.

Sometimes even the most highly respected "generals of the faith," like the beloved Dutch born Henri Nouwen, grow over time into that deep love for God that brings about pure trust. It is fascinating to me that when we look at Nouwen's first thirty nine books we find the word "faith" constantly referred to, but in his last book which was published the day he died, September 21, 1996, we find the word "faith" mentioned only once and the higher word "trust" talked about sixty five times.

So yes, we can be a Christian with only faith, and not have the <u>Ruthless Trust</u> that Brennan Manning discusses in his book of that name. But for us to have faith and not real trust is not what is commanded. It is not what God wants for our lives. And it is not what is best for us in every regard. In the end, as has been said, trust may be the only gift we can give to God. And in giving that gift we are truly set free.

We must strive for total trust. We must practice it

daily and try to perfect it. In the end, we must live it. It is the gift we give to God that gives so much more back to us. It is the one word that describes the ultimate Christian life.

No Fear, No Worry

We turn on the news today and in ten minutes are bombarded with upcoming worldwide economic catastrophe, the horror of impending nuclear problems from North Korea, Pakistan, or Iran, plus talk of food and water shortages unparalleled in human history. If that isn't enough we are frightened by pending doom from supposed disastrous climate change, or the uncertain peril of radical Islamic terrorist attacks. And all this is before the first commercial break, in which we are told about a new drug that will cure a disease we didn't even know existed, or are prodded to buy a new home protection system because a crazed murderer is sure to try to break into our home tonight. Is there any wonder that fear and worry are so common?

Knowing the precision of God's Word, though, I find it extremely interesting that the phrase, **"Do not fear"** is in the Bible 365 times. I guess that is once for every day of the year. Obviously fear is something that God does not want us to have, thus the constant reminder about it throughout the Bible.

Of course, "fear of the Lord" is a good thing. But in that respect "fear" actually means "awe". What we are not suppose to have is fear in the normal sense of the word. In 2 Timothy 1:7, the King James Version tells us, *"For God hath not given us the spirit of fear; but of power, and of love, and of a sound mind."* If fear is not given to us by God, it must come from Satan and his demons. And anything we have received from the Evil One must be rejected just as we need to reject Satan himself.

The same is true of worry, too. I am reminded of a story I heard years ago:

Death was walking toward a city one morning and a man asked, "What are you going to do?"

"I'm going to take ten people today," Death replied.

"That's horrible," the man said.

"That's the way it is ," Death said. "That's what I do."

The man hurried to warn everyone he could about Death's plan. As evening fell, he met Death again.

"You told me you were going to take ten people." the man said, "Why did a thousand die?"

"I kept my word," Death responded. "I only took ten people. Worry took the others ."

OK. So we know we are not to fear or worry, and it is easy to write or say that, but how do we accomplish it in real life? Is there something we can do that really works?

Years ago, when I had only been a born again Christian for a very few months, a wise and seasoned believer wrote a verse on his business card and advised me to memorize it. The verse was Proverbs 3:5-6, which says, ***"Trust in the Lord with all your heart and lean not on your own understanding; in all your ways acknowledge Him, and He will make your paths straight."***

Fortunately I went home that night and followed the man's advice. I committed the verse to memory. And I am so glad that I did. It has probably gone through my mind over a thousand times since then. I encourage you to do the same.

Did I immediately *"trust in the Lord with all my heart?"* Obviously, the answer is "no." But as the years rolled by and my walk with Jesus became closer and closer, I learned through his unfailing faithfulness that I could actually trust in Him completely, in every single aspect of my life. The same is true for anyone.

The startling thing is that once unequivocal trust in God is a true part of our being, when we do trust Christ completely with all our heart, not only do fear and worry vanish, but a phenomenal contentment describes our lives. In Hannah Whithall Smith's remarkable book from the mid 1800's, The Christian's Secret to a Happy Life, the bottom line of the secret of a happy life is unquestioning and grateful trust in God.

No, don't fear, don't worry, just trust. Ulcers are the badge of the untrusting Christian. Pure contentment and peace are the badges of the one who trusts.

Visits From Jesus

Something is happening in the world right now that is so phenomenal it is dumfounding that the media is not all over the story. Could it be that the "Prince of the air" is the prince of the "airwaves?" But that is another story. The story we need to pay attention to today can best be described by quoting verbatim what an extremely influential Saudi Islamic cleric, Sheikh Ahmad Al Qaraani, stated in a live interview on Aljazeera television. Al Qaraani lamented, **"In every hour, 667 Muslims convert to Christianity. Every day, 16,000 Muslims convert to Christianity."**

Think about what this Islamic leader said. This in itself is unprecedented. These Muslim converts are not like Joe American teenager who walks down an aisle at a church in Boise, Idaho, and then goes home to proud parents, grandparents, and Aunt Sue. Not at all. These Muslims convert with the full knowledge that they will be ostracized from their families and friends, persecuted, thrown in jail, possibly tortured, maybe even to death. Conversions from Islam to Christianity in decades past have been almost nonexistent because of these real life fears. Something huge has happened.

Part of it could be attributed to satellite TV, international radio evangelism, the disgust by moderate Muslims of extremist violence, or just the disenchantment caused by broken promises of Islamic government leaders. The big story is that these things, though, are not the main thing that drives the converts. The gigantic story that should be shouted from the rooftops is that these converts are having actual visits from Jesus Himself in the form of dreams and visions. These are not isolated cases. These are occurring and being documented by the thousands. And of the converts who have not had these awesome personal encounters with Christ, many are being converted by those who have.

As reported in Joel Rosenberg's wonderful nonfiction book, <u>Inside the Revolution</u>,

"An Iranian pastor I knew met a twenty-two year old Iranian Shia woman who had become a Christian after seeing a vision of Jesus Christ. She just showed up in his church one day hungry to study the Bible for herself. The more she studied God's word, the more deeply she loved Jesus. Soon she discovered that God had given her the spiritual gift of evangelism. ... Today she leads an average of fifteen people to Christ every day - that's right, *fifteen a day*. She told my pastor friend that Iranian Muslims are so desperate for the gospel that typically it takes about five minutes to share the story of her conversion and how God has changed her life before the listener is ready to also receive Christ. 'Difficult' conversations, she says, with several questions or concerns, take fifteen to twenty minutes."

Some of these real encounters with Jesus result in instructions to hear the good news from someone else. Rosenberg tells of one such case,

"One Iranian Muslim woman had a dream in which God told her, 'Whatever the two women you are going to meet with tomorrow tell you, listen to them.' Startled, she went through the next day curious who she would meet. … At one point two Iranian Christians came up to her and explained the message of salvation to her. She obeyed the Lord's direction from the dream, listened carefully, and then bowed her head and prayed to receive Christ as her Savior."

Another elderly Iranian woman was watching the *Jesus* film in Farsi on satellite TV. When she got to the end of it, she was in tears. The narrator of the film recited Jesus' words in Revelation 3:20, ***"Behold, I stand at the door and knock; if anyone hears my voice and opens the door, I will come in to him and dine with him, and he with Me."***

The woman decided she should open her door, and she literally walked over to her apartment door and opened it. As Rosenberg tells her story, "She was suddenly blinded by a bolt of light emanating from a figure in the doorway. 'Who is it?' she asked.

'It is I.' Jesus said.

'Come in, my Lord,' she said, and Jesus entered her home.

For the next few minutes, Jesus spoke to her about Himself, told her he loved her and had forgiven her, and told her to get a Bible and begin reading it. And then, as suddenly as he had appeared, He was gone." She, of course, gave her life to Christ.

But maybe these three women had already been leading exemplary lives. Is the awesome love of Christ being shown only to those types of Muslims? Not at all. A case in point was nicknamed, Jazaar, which means "butcher." Rosenberg calls him Saada. Here was a vicious terrorist who was friends with Yasser Arafat, his driver and bodyguard. He "happily" killed for Arafat and served as a sniper in the PLO. He had killed innocent Jews and Christians alike at one point.

"His friend began reading from the book of John, chapter one, verse one: 'In the beginning was the Word, and the Word was with God, and the Word was God.' … Saada began to shake. … Saada would later recall, 'Before I knew it I was on my knees. I didn't consciously decide to kneel. It just happened. I lost all awareness that my friend was in the room. A light came into my field of vision - a talking light. … The light said to me, "I am the Way, the Truth, and the Life. No one comes to the Father except through me." I didn't know at that moment that those words were what Jesus said during the Last Supper (in John 14:6). As far as I was concerned, they were a message from Jesus solely for me.

"Suddenly, Saada said, he just knew beyond the shadow of a doubt that the triune God - the Father, the Son, and the Holy Spirit - existed. He knew with certainty that this triune God loved him. and sobbing with shame at his sin and with thankfulness for God's mercy, he cried out, 'Oh Jesus, come into my life! Forgive me and be my Lord and Savior!" Reported by Joel Rosenberg,

Today Saada's passion is to bring the saving knowledge of Jesus to the Islamic world.

These are only a few of the thousands of true happenings in which Jesus Christ is visiting those in the Muslim world right now. Again I will say, this is unprecedented in these centuries. This is so extraordinary as to be indescribable. These are modern day Damascus Road experiences. And they are happening daily.

The burning question you and I need to ask is. "Why is Jesus leaving His seat beside the Father to enter the world through dreams and visions like He is today? Why now?" This is so utterly unusual and phenomenal, is there an unusual reason for it? I have my own opinion. Muse for a while and form your own. The answer is important.

A Last Musing

We have had a lot to muse about in this book. Mainly we have looked at the magnificence of both the Bible and God. Words can not describe or remotely do justice to either one. As to the Bible, I know that I have spent over 15,000 hours trying to learn about it, and have not even begun to scratch the surface. I am fully convinced that we will be studying it throughout the Millennial Reign of Christ, and we still may not uncover everything within its pages.

But when we muse about God, we are getting into an even more majestic and complex realm than even His Bible. He is utterly awesome in every aspect imaginable. There could be no subject we could spend our time studying that would ever be as fascinating as God. But at the heart of any study we might undertake concerning God, one thing will stand out, and that is His love for us, His children. Everything He has ever done, from the creation of everything, to the unseen blessing He just poured out in your life, was done because He loves you. That is the most awesome concept that we could ever ponder.

Of course, we are constantly in awe of His power, and the way He has orchestrated all of history to move mankind toward the desired goal, unity with Him. But probably what thrills me even more is to see the complex orchestration that goes into blessing us in some of the seemingly more minor areas of our lives. Such is the case in what may be my very favorite true God story of all time.

It occurred in Tallahassee, Florida, in 1955. Mary Helen Livingston was a young student nurse at Florida State College at the time. Her little boy, Bobby, was extremely ill. The doctor had explained to Mary that Bobby had to have fluids and had to eat. Mary had tried to follow the doctor's orders, but little Bobby couldn't keep anything down. His condition had gotten very serious, and Mary had no answers.

Then Bobby said, "Make me some shoo-fly pie, Mama. I could eat that. I know I could."

Mary had been reading Bobby stories about a little Amish boy who ate shoo-fly pie. She had no idea what was in it, but she decided she would find out and give it a try. Unfortunately, after calling every library and book store trying to find a recipe, all hope vanished. Remember, this was 1955, before computers and Google. Mary had tried everything she knew to do, and no-one she talked to could offer any suggestions either. Finally she explained the situation to Bobby and told him that she would go to the Winn Dixie grocery store and find something else.

"I'll ask God to send you a recipe there. He'll send you one." Bobby said.

All Mary could say was, "Oh no, Bobby, please don't do that." She didn't want his innocent faith shattered.

While in the Winn Dixie on Monroe Street, the highway to Thomasville, Georgia, two women walked in. one was wearing a black prayer cap, the other a white one, just like the pictures in Bobby's book. "Are you Amish?" Mary asked. They were, and of course they knew how to make Shoo-fly pie. Mary got her recipe and the ladies even helped find the ingredients.

When asked if they lived in Tallahassee, one lady replied, "Oh, goodness no! We were just passing through. We have been down in Florida and were on our way back home to Pennsylvania. I don't know why we came in here, but all of a sudden my companion said, 'Let's stop at Winn Dixie.' So here we are. I really don't know why."

Without having to muse very long, you and I know why. God is love. He loves us so much *"that He gave His only begotten Son, that whosoever believeth in Him should not perish, but have everlasting life."* John 3:16 (KJV).

He not only loves us that much, but He loves us enough to give a little boy shoo-fly pie.

About the Author
And Additional Books

Bob Morley graduated from the University of North Carolina with a degree in psychology in 1967. His vocation has been in sales management, primarily in the life insurance industry where his company, Christian Insurance Marketing, has agents in 35 states.

His passion, however, is God. This passion prompted over 15,000 hours in deep and rewarding study of our Creator and His Holy Word. That research has resulted in a blessing for many through his years of Christian writing.

Bob's highly acclaimed Unlocking God's Secrets may well be one of the best books ever written for bringing the lost into the Kingdom of God, while at the same time bringing existing believers into a richer relationship with their Savior, as well as giving them a much deeper understanding of the Bible. It is still available world wide through such fine book vendors as the one that brought Musings from Me and My Master to you. If you have not had the good fortune of reading it yet, please be encouraged to do so. It is a book you will never forget, and one that can be enjoyed over and over, uncovering new nuggets with each reading.

More information about Unlocking God's Secrets and Bob Morley is available at www.bobmorleybook.com or www.unlockinggodssecrets.com.

Bob and his wife, Barbara, reside in Greenville, S.C. Bob may be reached at morley120@juno.com.

Made in the USA
Charleston, SC
18 September 2010